Texas Rangers 2021

A Baseball Companion

Edited by Steven Goldman and Bret Sayre

Baseball Prospectus

Craig Brown, Associate Editor
Robert Au, Harry Pavlidis and Amy Pircher, Statistics Editors

Copyright © 2021 by DIY Baseball, LLC.
All rights reserved

This book or any part thereof may not be reproduced or transmitted in any form or by any means, electronic or mechanical, including photocopying, recording, or by any information storage and retrieval system, without permission in writing from the publisher.

Limit of Liability/Disclaimer of Warranty: While the publisher and the author have used their best efforts in preparing this book, they make no representations or warranties with respect to the accuracy or completeness of the contents of this book and specifically disclaim any implied warranties of merchantability or fitness for a particular purpose. No warranty may be created or extended by sales representatives or written sales materials. The advice and strategies contained herein may not be suitable for your situation. You should consult with a professional where appropriate. Neither the publisher nor the author shall be liable for any loss of profit or any other commercial damages, including but not limited to special, incidental, consequential, or other damages.

Library of Congress Cataloging-in-Publication Data:
paperback
ISBN-13: 978-1-950716-79-1

Project Credits
Cover Design: Ginny Searle
Interior Design and Production: Amy Pircher, Robert Au
Layout: Amy Pircher, Robert Au

Baseball icon courtesy of Uberux, from https://www.shareicon.net/author/uberux

Ballpark diagram courtesy of Lou Spirito/THIRTY81 Project, https://thirty81project.com/

Manufactured in the United States of America
10 9 8 7 6 5 4 3 2 1

Table of Contents

Statistical Introduction v

Part 1: Team Analysis

Performance Graphs 3
2020 Team Performance 4
2021 Team Projections 5
Team Personnel 6
Globe Life Park in Arlington Stats 7
Rangers Team Analysis 9

Part 2: Player Analysis

Rangers Player Analysis 14
Rangers Prospects 95

Part 3: Featured Articles

Rangers All-Time Top 10 Players 109
    by Steven Goldman

A Taxonomy of 2020 Abnormalities 115
    by Rob Mains

Tranches of WAR 121
    by Russell A. Carleton

Secondhand Sport 127
    by Patrick Dubuque

Steve Dalkowski Dreaming 131
    by Steven Goldman

A Reward For A Functioning Society 135
    by Cory Frontin and Craig Goldstein

Index of Names 139

Statistical Introduction

Sports are, fundamentally, a blend of athletic endeavor and storytelling. Baseball, like any other sport, tells its stories in so many ways: in the arc of a game from the stands or a season from the box scores, in photos, or even in numbers. At Baseball Prospectus, we understand that statistics don't replace observation or any of baseball's stories, but complement everything else that makes the game so much fun.

What stats help us with is with patterns and precision, variance and value. This book can help you learn things you may not see from watching a game or hundred, whether it's the path of a career over time or the breadth of the entire MLB. We'd also never ask you to choose between our numbers and the experience of viewing a game from the cheap seats or the comfort of your home; our publication combines running the numbers with observations and wisdom from some of the brightest minds we can find. But if you *do* want to learn more about the numbers beyond what's on the backs of player jerseys, let us help explain.

Offense

We've revised our methodology for determining batting value. Long-time readers of the book will notice that we've retired True Average in favor of a new metric: Deserved Runs Created Plus (DRC+). Developed by Jonathan Judge and our stats team, this statistic measures everything a player does at the plate–reaching base, hitting for power, making outs, and moving runners over–and puts it on a scale where 100 equals league-average performance. A DRC+ of 150 is terrific, a DRC+ of 100 is average and a DRC+ of 75 means you better be an excellent defender.

DRC+ also does a better job than any of our previous metrics in taking contextual factors into account. The model adjusts for how the park affects performance, but also for things like the talent of the opposing pitcher, value of different types of batted-ball events, league, temperature and other factors. It's able to describe a player's expected offensive contribution than any other statistic we've found over the years, and also does a better job of predicting future performance as well.

The other aspect of run-scoring is baserunning, which we quantify using Baserunning Runs. BRR not only records the value of stolen bases (or getting caught in the act), but also accounts for all the stuff that doesn't show up on the back of a baseball card: a runner's ability to go first to third on a single, or advance on a fly ball.

Defense

Where offensive value is *relatively* easy to identify and understand, defensive value is … not. Over the past dozen years, the sabermetric community has focused mostly on stats based on zone data: a real-live human person records the type of batted ball and estimated landing location, and models are created that give expected outs. From there, you can compare fielders' actual outs to those expected ones. Simple, right?

Unfortunately, zone data has two major issues. First, zone data is recorded by commercial data providers who keep the raw data private unless you pay for it. (All the statistics we build in this book and on our website use public data as inputs.) That hurts our ability to test assumptions or duplicate results. Second, over the years it has become apparent that there's quite a bit of "noise" in zone-based fielding analysis. Sometimes the conclusions drawn from zone data don't hold up to scrutiny, and sometimes the different data provided by different providers don't look anything alike, giving wildly different results. Sometimes the hard-working professional stringers or scorers might unknowingly inflict unconscious bias into the mix: for example good fielders will often be credited with more expected outs despite the data, and ballparks with high press boxes tend to score more line drives than ones with a lower press box.

Enter our Fielding Runs Above Average (FRAA). For most positions, FRAA is built from play-by-play data, which allows us to avoid the subjectivity found in many other fielding metrics. The idea is this: count how many fielding plays are made by a given player and compare that to expected plays for an average fielder at their position (based on pitcher ground ball tendencies and batter handedness). Then we adjust for park and base-out situations.

When it comes to catchers, our methodology is a little different thanks to the laundry list of responsibilities they're tasked with beyond just, well, catching and throwing the ball. By now you've probably heard about "framing" or the art of making umpires more likely to call balls outside the strike zone for strikes. To put this into one tidy number, we incorporate pitch tracking data (for the years it exists) and adjust for important factors like pitcher, umpire, batter and home-field advantage using a mixed-model approach. This grants us a number for how many strikes the catcher is personally adding to (or subtracting from) his pitchers' performance … which we then convert to runs added or lost using linear weights.

Framing is one of the biggest parts of determining catcher value, but we also take into account blocking balls from going past, whether a scorer deems it a passed ball or a wild pitch. We use a similar approach—one that really benefits from the pitch tracking data that tells us what ends up in the dirt and what doesn't. We also include a catcher's ability to prevent stolen bases and how well they field balls in play, and *finally* we come up with our FRAA for catchers.

Pitching

Both pitching and fielding make up the half of baseball that isn't run scoring: run prevention. Separating pitching from fielding is a tough task, and most recent pitching analysis has branched off from Voros McCracken's famous (and controversial) statement, "There is little if any difference among major-league pitchers in their ability to prevent hits on balls hit in the field of play." The research of the analytic community has validated this to some extent, and there are a host of "defense-independent" pitching measures that have been developed to try and extract the effect of the defense behind a hurler from the pitcher's work.

Our solution to this quandary is Deserved Run Average (DRA), our core pitching metric. DRA seeks to evaluate a pitcher's performance, much like earned run average (ERA), the tried-and-true pitching stat you've seen on every baseball broadcast or box score from the past century, but it's very different. To start, DRA takes an event-by-event look at what the pitchers does, and adjusts the value of that event based on different environmental factors like park, batter, catcher, umpire, base-out situation, run differential, inning, defense, home field advantage, pitcher role and temperature. That mixed model gives us a pitcher's expected contribution, similar to what we do for our DRC+ model for hitters and FRAA model for catchers. (Oh, and we also consider the pitcher's effect on basestealing and on balls getting past the catcher.)

DRA is set to the scale of runs allowed per nine innings (RA9) instead of ERA, which makes DRA's scale slightly higher than ERA's. Because of this, for ease of use, we're supplying DRA-, which is much easier for the reader to parse. As with DRC+, DRA- is an "index" stat, meaning instead of using some arbitrary and shifting number to denote what's "good," average is always 100. The reason that it uses a minus rather than a plus is because like ERA, a lower number is better. Therefore a 75 DRA- describes a performance 25 percent better than average, whereas a 150 DRA- means that either a pitcher is getting extremely lucky with their results, or getting ready to try a new pitch.

Since the last time you picked up an edition of this book, we've also made a few minor changes to DRA to make it better. Recent research into "tunneling"—the act of throwing consecutive pitches that appear similar from a batter's point of view until after the swing decision point–data has given us a new contextual factor to account for in DRA: plate distance. This refers to the distance between successive pitches as they approach the plate, and while it has a smaller effect than factors like velocity or whiff rate, it still can help explain pitcher strikeout rate in our model.

Recently Added Descriptive Statistics

Returning to our 2021 edition of the book are a few figures which recently appeared. These numbers may be a little bit more familiar to those of you who have spent some time investigating baseball statistics.

Fastball Percentage

Our fastball percentage (FA%) statistic measures how frequently a pitcher throws a pitch classified as a "fastball," measured as a percentage of overall pitches thrown. We qualify three types of fastballs:

1. The traditional four-seam fastball;
2. The two-seam fastball or sinker;
3. "Hard cutters," which are pitches that have the movement profile of a cut fastball and are used as the pitcher's primary offering or in place of a more traditional fastball.

For example, a pitcher with a FA% of 67 throws any combination of these three pitches about two-thirds of the time.

Whiff Rate

Everybody loves a swing and a miss, and whiff rate (Whiff%) measures how frequently pitchers induce a swinging strike. To calculate Whiff%, we add up all the pitches thrown that ended with a swinging strike, then divide that number by a pitcher's total pitches thrown. Most often, high whiff rates correlate with high strikeout rates (and overall effective pitcher performance).

Called Strike Probability

Called Strike Probability (CSP) is a number that represents the likelihood that all of a pitcher's pitches will be called a strike while controlling for location, pitcher and batter handedness, umpire and count. Here's how it works: on each pitch, our model determines how many times (out of 100) that a similar pitch was called for a strike given those factors mentioned above, and when normalized for each batter's strike zone. Then we average the CSP for all pitches thrown by a pitcher in a season, and that gives us the yearly CSP percentage you see in the stats boxes.

As you might imagine, pitchers with a higher CSP are more likely to work in the zone, where pitchers with a lower CSP are likely locating their pitches outside the normal strike zone, for better or for worse.

Projections

Many of you aren't turning to this book just for a look at what a player has done, but for a look at what a player is going to do: the PECOTA projections. PECOTA, initially developed by Nate Silver (who has moved on to greater fame as a political analyst), consists of three parts:

1. Major-league equivalencies, which use minor-league statistics to project how a player will perform in the major leagues;
2. Baseline forecasts, which use weighted averages and regression to the mean to estimate a player's current true talent level; and
3. Aging curves, which uses the career paths of comparable players to estimate how a player's statistics are likely to change over time.

With all those important things covered, let's take a look at what's in the book this year.

Team Prospectus

Most of this book is composed of team chapters, with one for each of the 30 major-league franchises. On the first page of each chapter, you'll see a box that contains some of the key statistics for each team as well as a very inviting stadium diagram.

We start with the team name, their unadjusted 2020 win-loss record, and their divisional ranking. Beneath that are a host of other team statistics. **Pythag** presents an adjusted 2020 winning percentage, calculated by taking runs scored per game (**RS/G**) and runs allowed per game (**RA/G**) for the team, and running them through a version of Bill James' Pythagorean formula that was refined and improved by David Smyth and Brandon Heipp. (The formula is called "Pythagenpat," which is equally fun to type and to say.)

Next up is **DRC+**, described earlier, to indicate the overall hitting ability of the team either above or below league-average. Run prevention on the pitching side is covered by **DRA** (also mentioned earlier) and another metric: Fielding Independent Pitching (**FIP**), which calculates another ERA-like statistic based on strikeouts, walks, and home runs recorded. Defensive Efficiency Rating (**DER**) tells us the percentage of balls in play turned into outs for the team, and is a quick fielding shorthand that rounds out run prevention.

After that, we have several measures related to roster composition, as opposed to on-field performance. **B-Age** and **P-Age** tell us the average age of a team's batters and pitchers, respectively. **Payroll** is the combined team payroll for all on-field players, and Doug Pappas' Marginal Dollars per Marginal Win (**M$/MW**) tells us how much money a team spent to earn production above replacement level.

Next to each of these stats, we've listed each team's MLB rank in that category from first to 30th. In this, first always indicates a positive outcome and 30th a negative outcome, except in the case of salary—first is highest.

After the franchise statistics, we share a few items about the team's home ballpark. There's the aforementioned diagram of the park's dimensions (including distances to the outfield wall), a graphic showing the height of the wall from the left-field pole to the right-field pole, and a table showing three-year park factors for the stadium. The park factors are displayed as indexes where 100 is average, 110 means that the park inflates the statistic in question by 10 percent, and 90 means that the park deflates the statistic in question by 10 percent.

On the second page of each team chapter, you'll find three graphs. The first is **Payroll History** and helps you see how the team's payroll has compared to the MLB and divisional average payrolls over time. Payroll figures are current as of January 1, 2021; with so many free agents still unsigned as of this writing, the final 2021 figure will likely be significantly different for many teams. (In the meantime, you can always find the most current data at Baseball Prospectus' Cot's Baseball Contracts page.)

The second graph is **Future Commitments** and helps you see the team's future outlays, if any.

The third graph is **Farm System Ranking** and displays how the Baseball Prospectus prospect team has ranked the organization's farm system since 2007.

After the graphs, we have a **Personnel** section that lists many of the important decision-makers and upper-level field and operations staff members for the franchise, as well as any former Baseball Prospectus staff members who are currently part of the organization. (In very rare circumstances, someone might be on both lists!)

Position Players

After all that information and a thoughtful bylined essay covering each team, we present our player comments. These are also bylined, but due to frequent franchise shifts during the offseason, our bylines are more a rough guide than a perfect accounting of who wrote what.

Each player is listed with the major-league team that employed him as of early January 2021. If a player changed teams after that point via free agency, trade, or any other method, you'll be able to find them in the chapter for their previous squad.

As an example, take a look at the player comment for Padres shortstop Fernando Tatis Jr.: the stat block that accompanies his written comment is at the top of this page. First we cover biographical information (age is as of June 30, 2021) before moving onto the stats themselves. Our statistic columns include standard identifying information like **YEAR**, **TEAM**, **LVL** (level of affiliated play) and **AGE** before getting into the numbers. Next, we provide raw, untranslated

Fernando Tatis Jr. SS
Born: 01/02/99   Age: 22   Bats: R   Throws: R
Height: 6'3"   Weight: 217   Origin: International Free Agent, 2015

YEAR	TEAM	LVL	AGE	PA	R	2B	3B	HR	RBI	BB	K	SB	CS	AVG/OBP/SLG
2018	SA	AA	19	394	77	22	4	16	43	33	109	16	5	.286/.355/.507
2019	SD	MLB	20	372	61	13	6	22	53	30	110	16	6	.317/.379/.590
2020	SD	MLB	21	257	50	11	2	17	45	27	61	11	3	.277/.366/.571
2021 FS	SD	MLB	22	600	95	24	4	31	81	50	165	17	8	.263/.331/.499
2021 DC	SD	MLB	22	628	100	25	4	32	85	53	173	19	8	.263/.331/.499

Comparables: Darryl Strawberry, Bo Bichette, Ronald Acuña Jr.

YEAR	TEAM	LVL	AGE	PA	DRC+	BABIP	BRR	FRAA	WARP
2018	SA	AA	19	394	136	.370	3.0	SS(83): -1.9	2.4
2019	SD	MLB	20	372	118	.410	7.1	SS(83): 0.9	3.4
2020	SD	MLB	21	257	126	.306	0.7	SS(57): -5.5	0.9
2021 FS	SD	MLB	22	600	126	.318	1.7	SS -1	3.9
2021 DC	SD	MLB	22	628	126	.318	1.8	SS -1	4.0

numbers like you might find on the back of your dad's baseball cards: **PA** (plate appearances), **R** (runs), **2B** (doubles), **3B** (triples), **HR** (home runs), **RBI** (runs batted in), **BB** (walks), **K** (strikeouts), **SB** (stolen bases) and **CS** (caught stealing).

Following the basic stats is **Whiff%** (whiff rate), which denotes how often, when a batter swings, he fails to make contact with the ball. Another way to think of this number is an inverse of a hitter's contact rate.

Next, we have unadjusted "slash" statistics: **AVG** (batting average), **OBP** (on-base percentage) and **SLG** (slugging percentage). Following the slash line is **DRC+** (Deserved Runs Created Plus), which we described earlier as total offensive expected contribution compared to the league average.

BABIP (batting average on balls in play) tells us how often a ball in play fell for a hit, and can help us identify whether a batter may have been lucky or not ... but note that high BABIPs also tend to follow the great hitters of our time, as well as speedy singles hitters who put the ball on the ground.

The next item is **BRR** (Baserunning Runs), which covers all of a player's baserunning accomplishments including (but not limited to) swiped bags and failed attempts. Next is **FRAA** (Fielding Runs Above Average), which also includes the number of games previously played at each position noted in parentheses. Multi-position players have only their two most frequent positions listed here, but their total FRAA number reflects all positions played.

Our last column here is **WARP** (Wins Above Replacement Player). WARP estimates the total value of a player, which means for hitters it takes into account hitting runs above average (calculated using the DRC+ model), BRR and FRAA. Then, it makes an adjustment for positions played and gives the player a credit for plate appearances based upon the difference between "replacement level"—which is derived from the quality of players added to a team's roster after the start of the season–and the league average.

The final line just below the stats box is **PECOTA** data, which is discussed further in a following section.

Catchers

Catchers are a special breed, and thus they have earned their own separate box which displays some of the defensive metrics that we've built just for them. As an example, let's check out Yasmani Grandal.

YEAR	TEAM	P. COUNT	FRM RUNS	BLK RUNS	THRW RUNS	TOT RUNS
2018	LAD	16816	15.7	0.8	0.1	16.5
2019	MIL	18740	19.4	1.8	-0.1	21.1
2020	CHW	4830	3.7	0.3	-0.2	3.8
2021	CHW	14430	16.7	-0.6	1.0	17.1
2021	CHW	14430	16.7	0.4	1.0	18.0

The **YEAR** and **TEAM** columns match what you'd find in the other stat box. **P. COUNT** indicates the number of pitches thrown while the catcher was behind the plate, including swinging strikes, fouls and balls in play. **FRM RUNS** is the total run value the catcher provided (or cost) his team by influencing the umpire to call strikes where other catchers did not. **BLK RUNS** expresses the total run value above or below average for the catcher's ability to prevent wild pitches and passed balls. **THRW RUNS** is calculated using a similar model as the previous two statistics, and it measures a catcher's ability to throw out basestealers but also to dissuade them from testing his arm in the first place. It takes into account factors like the pitcher (including his delivery and pickoff move) and baserunner (who could be as fast as Billy Hamilton or as slow as Yonder Alonso). **TOT RUNS** is the sum of all of the previous three statistics.

Pitchers

Let's give our pitchers a turn, using 2020 AL Cy Young winner Shane Bieber as our example. Take a look at his stat block: the first line and the **YEAR**, **TEAM**, **LVL** and **AGE** columns are the same as in the position player example earlier.

Here too, we have a series of columns that display raw, unadjusted statistics compiled by the pitcher over the course of a season: **W** (wins), **L** (losses), **SV** (saves), **G** (games pitched), **GS** (games started), **IP** (innings pitched), **H** (hits allowed) and **HR** (home runs allowed). Next we have two statistics that are rates: **BB/9** (walks per nine innings) and **K/9** (strikeouts per nine innings), before returning to the unadjusted **K** (strikeouts).

Next up is **GB%** (ground ball percentage), which is the percentage of all batted balls that were hit on the ground, including both outs and hits. Remember, this is based on observational data and subject to human error, so please approach this with a healthy dose of skepticism.

BABIP (batting average on balls in play) is calculated using the same methodology as it is for position players, but it often tells us more about a pitcher than it does a hitter. With pitchers, a high BABIP is often due to poor defense or bad luck, and can often be an indicator of potential rebound, and a low BABIP may be cause to expect performance regression. (A typical league-average BABIP is close to .290-.300.)

The metrics **WHIP** (walks plus hits per inning pitched) and **ERA** (earned run average) are old standbys: WHIP measures walks and hits allowed on a per-inning basis, while ERA measures earned runs on a nine-inning basis. Neither of these stats are translated or adjusted.

DRA- (Deserved Run Average) was described at length earlier, and measures how the pitcher "deserved" to perform compared to other pitchers. Please note that since we lack all the data points that would make for a "real" DRA for minor-league events, the DRA- displayed for minor league partial-seasons is based off of different data. (That data is a modified version of our cFIP metric, which you can find more information about on our website.)

Shane Bieber   RHP

Born: 05/31/95   Age: 26   Bats: R   Throws: R
Height: 6'3"   Weight: 200   Origin: Round 4, 2016 Draft (#122 overall)

YEAR	TEAM	LVL	AGE	W	L	SV	G	GS	IP	H	HR	BB/9	K/9	K	GB%	BABIP
2018	AKR	AA	23	3	0	0	5	5	31	26	1	0.3	8.7	30	47.3%	.278
2018	COL	AAA	23	3	1	0	8	8	48^2	30	3	1.1	8.7	47	52.0%	.227
2018	CLE	MLB	23	11	5	0	20	19	114^2	130	13	1.8	9.3	118	46.2%	.356
2019	CLE	MLB	24	15	8	0	34	33	214^1	186	31	1.7	10.9	259	44.4%	.298
2020	CLE	MLB	25	8	1	0	12	12	77^1	46	7	2.4	14.2	122	48.4%	.267
2021 FS	CLE	MLB	26	10	6	0	26	26	150	121	18	2.1	11.7	195	45.5%	.297
2021 DC	CLE	MLB	26	14	7	0	30	30	196.7	159	24	2.1	11.7	257	45.5%	.297

Comparables: Luis Severino, Danny Salazar, Joe Musgrove

YEAR	TEAM	LVL	AGE	WHIP	ERA	DRA-	WARP	MPH	FB%	WHF	CSP
2018	AKR	AA	23	0.87	1.16	61	0.9				
2018	COL	AAA	23	0.74	1.66	69	1.2				
2018	CLE	MLB	23	1.33	4.55	74	2.6	94.7	57.4%	26.2%	
2019	CLE	MLB	24	1.05	3.28	75	4.9	94.4	45.8%	30.8%	
2020	CLE	MLB	25	0.87	1.63	53	2.6	95.3	53.6%	40.7%	
2021 FS	CLE	MLB	26	1.04	2.44	64	4.4	94.7	50.0%	33.2%	44.2%
2021 DC	CLE	MLB	26	1.04	2.44	64	5.8	94.7	50.0%	33.2%	44.2%

Just like with hitters, **WARP** (Wins Above Replacement Player) is a total value metric that puts pitchers of all stripes on the same scale as position players. We use DRA as the primary input for our calculation of WARP. You might notice that relief pitchers (due to their limited innings) may have a lower WARP than you were expecting or than you might see in other WARP-like metrics. WARP does not take leverage into account, just the actions a pitcher performs and the expected value of those actions ... which ends up judging high-leverage relief pitchers differently than you might imagine given their prestige and market value.

MPH gives you the pitcher's 95th percentile velocity for the noted season, in order to give you an idea of what the *peak* fastball velocity a pitcher possesses. Since this comes from our pitch-tracking data, it is not publicly available for minor-league pitchers.

Finally, we display the three new pitching metrics we described earlier. **FB%** (fastball percentage) gives you the percentage of fastballs thrown out of all pitches. **WHF** (whiff rate) tells you the percentage of swinging strikes induced out of all pitches. **CSP** (called strike probability) expresses the likelihood of all pitches thrown to result in a called strike, after controlling for factors like handedness, umpire, pitch type, count and location.

PECOTA

All players have PECOTA projections for 2021, as well as a set of other numbers that describe the performance of comparable players according to PECOTA. All projections for 2021 are for the player at the date we went to press in early January and are projected into the league and park context as indicated by the team abbreviation. (Note that players at very low levels of the minors are too unpredictable to assess using these numbers.) All PECOTA projected statistics represent a player's projected major-league performance.

How we're doing that is a little different this season. There are really two different values that go into the final stat line that you see for PECOTA: How a player performs, and how much playing time he'll be given to perform it. In the past we've estimated playing time based on each team's roster and depth charts, and we'll continue to do that. These projections are denoted as **2021 DC**.

But in many cases, a player won't be projected for major-league playing time; most of the time this is because they aren't projected to be major-league players at all, but still developing as prospects. Or perhaps a player will provide Triple-A depth, only to have an opportunity open up because of injury. For these purposes, we're also supplying a second projection, labeled **2021 FS**, or full season. This is what we would project the player to provide in 600 plate appearances or 150 innings pitched.

Below the projections are the player's three highest-scoring comparable players as determined by PECOTA. All comparables represent a snapshot of how the listed player was performing at the same age as the current player, so if a

23-year-old pitcher is compared to Bartolo Colón, he's actually being compared to a 23-year-old Colón, not the version that pitched for the Rangers in 2018, nor to Colón's career as a whole.

A few points about pitcher projections. First, we aren't yet projecting peak velocity, so that column will be blank in the PECOTA lines. Second, projecting DRA is trickier than evaluating past performance, because it is unclear how deserving each pitcher will be of his anticipated outcomes. However, we know that another DRA-related statistic–contextual FIP or cFIP-estimates future run scoring very well. So for PECOTA, the projected DRA- figures you see are based on the past cFIPs generated by the pitcher and comparable players over time, along with the other factors described above.

If you're familiar with PECOTA, then you'll have noticed that the projection system often appears bullish on players coming off a bad year and bearish on players coming off a good year. (This is because the system weights several previous seasons, not just the most recent one.) In addition, we publish the 50th percentile projections for each player–which is smack in the middle of the range of projected production—which tends to mean PECOTA stat lines don't often have extreme results like 40 home runs or 250 strikeouts in a given season. In essence, PECOTA doesn't project very many extreme seasons.

Managers

After all those wonderful team chapters, we've got statistics for each big-league manager, all of whom are organized by alphabetical order. Here you'll find a block including an extraordinary amount of information collected from each manager's entire career. For more information on the acronyms and what they mean, please visit the Glossary at www.baseballprospectus.com.

There is one important metric that we'd like to call attention to, and you'll find it next to each manager's name: **wRM+** (weighted reliever management plus). Developed by Rob Arthur and Rian Watt, wRM+ investigates how good a manager is at using their best relievers during the moments of highest leverage, using both our proprietary DRA metric as well as Leverage Index. wRM+ is scaled to a league average of 100, and a wRM+ of 105 indicates that relievers were used approximately five percent "better" than average. On the other hand, a wRM+ of 95 would tell us the team used its relievers five percent "worse" than the average team.

While wRM+ does not have an extremely strong correlation with a manager, it is statistically significant; this means that a manager is not *entirely* responsible for a team's wRM+, but does have some effect on that number.

Part 1: Team Analysis

Performance Graphs

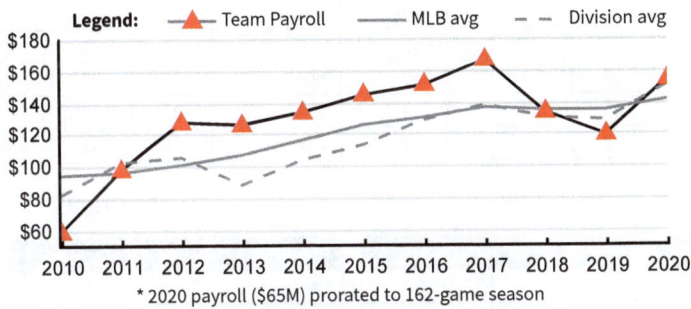

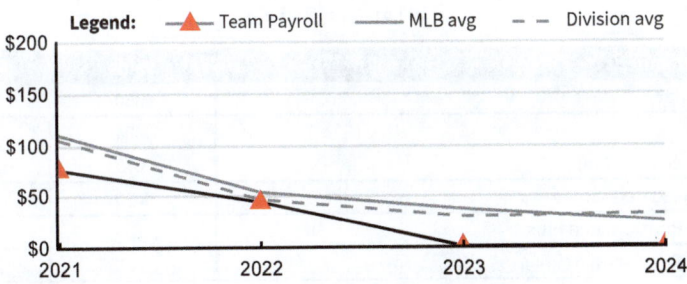

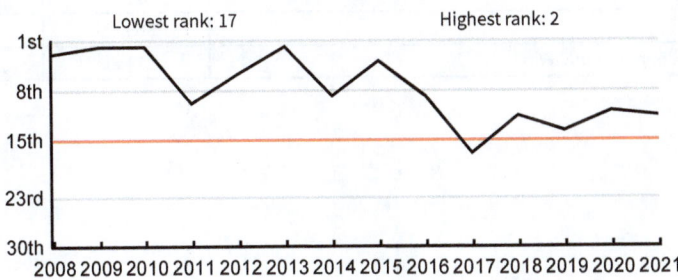

2020 Team Performance

ACTUAL STANDINGS

Team	W	L	Pct
OAK	36	24	0.600
HOU	29	31	0.483
SEA	27	33	0.450
LAA	26	34	0.433
TEX	22	38	0.367

dWIN% STANDINGS

Team	W	L	Pct
OAK	29	31	0.499
LAA	29	31	0.497
HOU	28	32	0.472
SEA	22	38	0.370
TEX	18	42	0.304

TOP HITTERS

Player	WARP
Joey Gallo	0.8
Leody Taveras	0.4
Jose Trevino	0.4

TOP PITCHERS

Player	WARP
Lance Lynn	0.9
Jonathan Hernández	0.5
Joely Rodríguez	0.3

VITAL STATISTICS

Statistic Name	Value	Rank
Pythagenpat	.350	30th
dWin%	.304	30th
Runs Scored per Game	3.73	29th
Runs Allowed per Game	5.20	26th
Deserved Runs Created Plus	83	30th
Deserved Run Average Minus	111	25th
Fielding Independent Pitching	4.92	22nd
Defensive Efficiency Rating	.708	6th
Batter Age	27.9	3rd
Pitcher Age	29.3	20th
Payroll	$65.0M	12th
Marginal $ per Marginal Win	$11.8M	30th

2021 Team Projections

PROJECTED STANDINGS

Team	W	L	Pct	+/-
HOU	92.5	69.5	0.571	14
There's reason to be skeptical of the starting pitching depth, but this team will score plenty of runs.				
LAA	86.2	75.8	0.532	16
Still buying pitching from the bargain bin despite a new GM, they lack the depth to be great, but if the stars stay healthy, they'll be good.				
OAK	82.2	79.8	0.507	-15
Free-agent departures in the outfield, infield, and bullpen leave them scrambling for coverage despite Matts Chapman and Olson.				
SEA	70.7	91.3	0.436	-2
The rebuild should be nearly over, but will go on for at least another year after a shockingly silent winter.				
TEX	**66.8**	**95.2**	**0.412**	**7**
A team in total, chaotic transition, but the kids could be fun to watch.				

TOP PROJECTED HITTERS

Player	WARP
Joey Gallo	3.1
Nick Solak	2.8
Willie Calhoun	1.2

TOP PROJECTED PITCHERS

Player	WARP
Kohei Arihara	1.8
Dane Dunning	1.5
Kyle Gibson	1.5

FARM SYSTEM REPORT

Top Prospect	Number of Top 101 Prospects
Leody Taveras, #26	4

KEY DEDUCTIONS

Player	WARP
Lance Lynn	2.7
Corey Kluber	2.4
Elvis Andrus	1.3
Rafael Montero	0.7

KEY ADDITIONS

Player	WARP
Kohei Arihara	1.8
Dane Dunning	1.5
Mike Foltynewicz	1.3
David Dahl	1.1
Nate Lowe	1.0
Khris Davis	0.6
Josh Sborz	0.3
Jonah Heim	0.3

Team Personnel

President of Baseball Operations
Jon Daniels

Executive Vice President & General Manager
Chris Young

Assistant General Manager
Josh Boyd

Assistant General Manager
Mike Daly

Assistant General Manager
Shiraz Rehman

Manager
Chris Woodward

BP Alumni
Bradley Ankrom

Globe Life Park in Arlington Stats

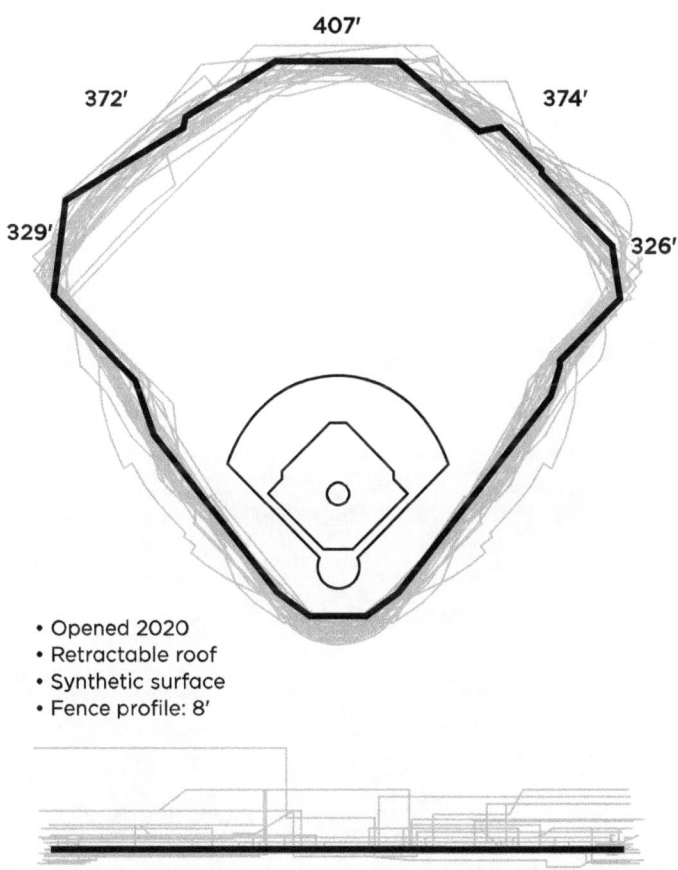

- Opened 2020
- Retractable roof
- Synthetic surface
- Fence profile: 8'

Three-Year Park Factors

Runs	Runs/RH	Runs/LH	HR/RH	HR/LH
109	108	111	103	106

Rangers Team Analysis

"**Y**eah, they did me dirty with the picture here."
Rangers slugger Joey Gallo is unhappy with his photos in *MLB The Show*, the popular baseball video game series. "Let's look at it again," he says to his live stream audience on Twitch. Gallo flips through flattering headshots and action variants of his teammates Mike Minor and Elvis Andrus. The selected images ooze competence and charisma. When Gallo finds himself in the game, competence turns to comedy. The first photo shows Gallo at the end of his swing, but his face tells a different story. With his head tilted towards the sky, eyes closed, and mouth agape, he appears to be belting a Mariah Carey high note. "Why in the hell did they think that THIS would be a good picture to put for me?" The second photo, a close-up, shows the slugger staring down the camera with a deranged expression. The face of the franchise has become an embarrassing mugshot.

The video clip of Gallo's flabbergasted reaction has been viewed 138,000 times. The act of live streaming a video game to viewers may seem foreign to some, but in the weeks after spring training was shut down, it became a form of fan outreach. Representatives from all 30 teams flocked to the live streaming platform Twitch.TV and put together the *MLB The Show* Players League, a tournament in which ballplayers faced off against each other as their digital counterparts. Some of baseball's brightest stars, like Fernando Tatís Jr. and Juan Soto, were participants. The competition drummed up plenty of goodwill for Gallo, who led Texas to the playoffs with a 23-6 record. Sadly, the Rangers' success on PlayStation did not translate to real life.

In many ways, Gallo's experience with *The Show* mirrored the feelings of many Rangers fans in 2020. Their new stadium sat empty, and the promise of a franchise to supply a team worthy of its energy fell through. But it's not uncommon for either video games or baseball teams to fail to deliver the experience described on the back of the box.

⚾ ⚾ ⚾

It's a little jarring to revisit the early concept art detailing Globe Life Field, the theoretical new home of the Rangers. The sun bleached pastels of 2019 feel downright Rockwellian a year later, and the concourses and pavilions are teeming with (photoshopped) life, crowds and activities. It's designed to look like an open-air playground, a permanent summer day; it's also designed to deserve the millions in public money devoted to the city's third stadium in half a century.

The new ballpark lacks the grandeur of its neighbor, AT&T Stadium, home of the Dallas Cowboys. AT&T, better known colloquially as "Jerry World" after Cowboys owner Jerry Jones, is the stadium equivalent of a gaudy McMansion. And if Jerry World is a mansion, the newly constructed Globe Life Field is the metal shed in the backyard. It's a *very* nice shed, but it's still a shed. When construction was complete, fans found it to be quite understated compared to the initial renderings. One common complaint was that the stadium's interior was dimmer and gloomier than expected. The effect was in part due to a foreign concept, and one that necessitated the building altogether: a retractable metal roof, a belated solution to the common 100-plus degree three-plus hour games of August.

When Globe Life Park was approved in 2016, the Rangers had tremendous aspirations, envisioning themselves as a franchise immune to the ebbs and flows of competitive cycles. The team was en route to its fifth playoff appearance in seven tries, and 90-win seasons were becoming an expectation. Meanwhile, the farm system looked strong, in part because the team relied more on international signings than draft choices. Joey Gallo, Nomar Mazara, Dillon Tate and Lewis Brinson led a prospect class ready to reinforce the existing nucleus of Elvis Andrus, Rougned Odor, and the healthy-any-day-now former number-one prospect Jurickson Profar. They headlined a generation that was expected to continue the Rangers' winning ways, effortlessly replacing the production of players like Adrián Beltré, Josh Hamilton and Ian Kinsler.

That second prospect wave never materialized. Brinson was traded to Milwaukee before his big-league debut, while Profar and Mazara were eventually shipped off after failing to reach stardom. Gallo remains with the Rangers, where a .253/.389/.598 slash line in his injury-shortened 2019 campaign made him into a dark horse MVP candidate. In 2020, Gallo's DRC+ fell from 128 to 84, as his exit velocity dipped and his line drives started hanging in the air. Leody Taveras, the last surviving member of that 2016 class, finally made his debut (at the age of 21) and hit like a 21-year-old. The offense-oriented prospects the team acquired in trade, Nick Solak and Willie Calhoun, failed to provide any offense. Ronald Guzmán was the lone regular to post a league-average OPS, and then only barely; he subsequently lost his job when the team acquired Nate Lowe in the offseason. Only a final-series sweep prevented them from earning next year's first-overall draft pick.

While the prospects haven't panned out as expected, they've also struggled to attract big name free agents. As the opening of the new ballpark grew closer, Texas kept tabs on the likes of Bryce Harper, Manny Machado and Gerrit Cole, but wasn't hyper-competitive for their services. The Rangers front office came closest to making a splash signing with Anthony Rendon, a Texas native. A free agent's market is typically dictated by how many years teams are willing to offer. The Los Angeles Angels offered Rendon a fully guaranteed seven-year deal worth $245 million. The Rangers' offer? Six years plus an option. In a moment of candor, Rangers GM Jon Daniels simply stated "I'm not going to sugar coat it: It sucks," in response to barely missing out on Rendon.

The long-tenured Daniels has now been promoted to Director of Baseball Operations, with former pitcher Chris Young taking over as the club's general manager. The task ahead of them is a difficult one: How to market a team without a star, or a core. Daniels has made some shrewd mid-level signings, perhaps none better than Lance Lynn for three years and $30 million, but despite the brand new $1.2 billion stadium and the fifth-largest media market in the country, austerity has defined the Rangers' approach to free agency and player salaries. The organization can split the cost of a new ballpark with Arlington's taxpayers, but the cost of an elite third baseman like Rendon falls squarely on the shoulders of ownership.

The 2020 season was an unmitigated disaster on the field, but it also may have been a blessing for the franchise, a jolt heavy enough to dislodge the team from its doldrums. Daniels and Young appear to have finally committed to a full rebuild. The team held on to Lynn at last year's deadline, but with a year remaining on his contract, the Rangers sent him to the White Sox for a promising arm in Dane Dunning. Andrus, whose bat and glove have both slipped, was formally demoted, and Gold Glover Isiah Kiner-Falefa has been anointed the team's starting shortstop.

From here the marketing gets easier; after all, major-league teams have been selling the hard rebuild as a philosophy for a decade now. It starts with the kids. Even if the future isn't ready in 2021, a future is ready: Sam Huff, Sherten Apostel and Anderson Tejeda all made the jump from High-A to the majors last year; along with the post-hype prospects of 2020, they'll combine to form one of the youngest offenses in the league. The kids won't have to play well, at least not all the time; they just have to play, and do something amazing once in a while to stitch into the television commercials. On the off days, there's always an opportunity to hint at the exit velocity of Bayron Lora or hype up top prospect Josh Jung. It's easy to sell the future, especially when everyone would like to forget the present.

It may not even be all false advertising. Taveras could lock down center field, making adjustments in his second tour of the majors. Solak could finally be the man to displace Odor as Kiner-Falefa did to Andrus. Free agent leftovers Kyle Gibson and Jordan Lyles could provide the team value by pitching well enough to pitch elsewhere, and Kolby Allard and Kyle Cody could continue making progress. It's probably a pipe dream, but people like pipe dreams. The Rangers are the concept art of baseball teams.

Texas Rangers 2021

Reclaiming their new ballpark in front of their home fans will be a welcome start. Globe Life Field was the reluctant star of the 2020 postseason, as the home of the Rangers became the guest house of the World Series champion Dodgers. It's telling that the current Globe Life Field home run leader isn't a Texas Ranger, but rather Corey Seager. The Dodgers didn't just make themselves at home. They kept their boots on and tracked mud all over the carpets. Texas fans were left to squint at the blue jerseys on their televisions and imagine what it would be like for their own players to make those home run-saving grabs.

⚾ ⚾ ⚾

A few days after his viral outburst, Joey Gallo logs into *MLB The Show* on his PlayStation. Per his request, the game's developers have updated his in-game photos. He now appears as a competent athlete capable of striking fear in his opponents. Optimistic Rangers fans will wait for their beloved franchise to receive its own patch, so that they can be portrayed in a more flattering light in the years to come. The pessimists will note that they've been making these games since Ian Kinsler was a rookie, and they never quite get out all the bugs.

—*Bailey Freeman is the creator of the Youtube channel Foolish Baseball.*

Part 2: Player Analysis

PLAYER COMMENTS WITH GRAPHS

Willie Calhoun LF
Born: 11/04/94   Age: 26   Bats: L   Throws: R
Height: 5'8"   Weight: 200   Origin: Round 4, 2015 Draft (#132 overall)

YEAR	TEAM	LVL	AGE	PA	R	2B	3B	HR	RBI	BB	K	SB	CS	AVG/OBP/SLG
2018	RR	AAA	23	469	66	32	0	9	47	32	47	4	0	.295/.352/.432
2018	TEX	MLB	23	108	8	5	0	2	11	6	24	0	0	.222/.269/.333
2019	NAS	AAA	24	172	23	8	0	8	28	32	24	1	1	.297/.433/.529
2019	TEX	MLB	24	337	51	14	1	21	48	23	53	0	0	.269/.323/.524
2020	TEX	MLB	25	108	3	2	1	1	13	5	17	0	0	.190/.231/.260
2021 FS	TEX	MLB	26	600	73	31	2	24	74	45	108	0	0	.252/.318/.452
2021 DC	TEX	MLB	26	548	66	28	2	22	68	41	98	0	0	.252/.318/.452

Comparables: Ozzie Timmons, Kevin Mitchell, Kevin Mench

When thinking about Calhoun's early big-league career, the word snakebit jumps out. How else to describe a year's worth of plate appearances, spread over four years of tumult? In the words of the Rolling Stones (and lots of car commercials), you can't always get what you want. After a first couple of seasons filled with more starts and stops than a traffic jam on I-20, it looked like Calhoun finally locked down an everyday role, breaking through with a 2019 campaign where he launched 14 dingers in his last 52 games. That all came to a screeching halt with an errant 95-mph fastball to the jaw from Julio Urías in spring training. While the fractured jaw was obviously bad, the psychological impact remained long after the bones had knitted. Calhoun himself admitted to skittishness when facing left-handed pitching. The Rangers brought him along slowly against lefties, and after that kind of trauma, it might take awhile for Calhoun to regain his comfort. It's another speed bump in his ascension, but let's hope time is on his side.

YEAR	TEAM	LVL	AGE	PA	DRC+	BABIP	BRR	FRAA	WARP
2018	RR	AAA	23	469	119	.315	-3.2	LF(91): -11.9	0.0
2018	TEX	MLB	23	108	86	.267	-0.7	LF(27): -2.8	-0.3
2019	NAS	AAA	24	172	141	.311	-0.8	LF(33): -6.5, 2B(3): 0.2	0.6
2019	TEX	MLB	24	337	118	.262	1.1	LF(71): -7.1	1.1
2020	TEX	MLB	25	108	76	.214	-1.2	LF(8): -0.0	-0.2
2021 FS	TEX	MLB	26	600	104	.276	-0.9	LF -1, 2B 0	1.6
2021 DC	TEX	MLB	26	548	104	.276	-0.8	LF -1	1.2

Willie Calhoun, continued

Batted Ball Distribution

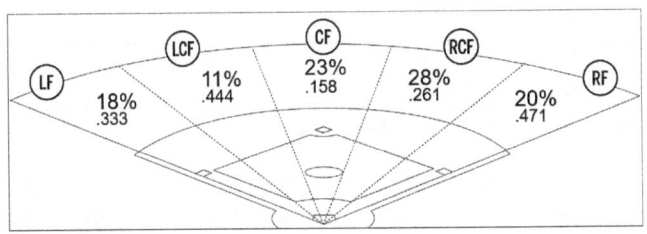

Strike Zone vs LHP   Strike Zone vs RHP

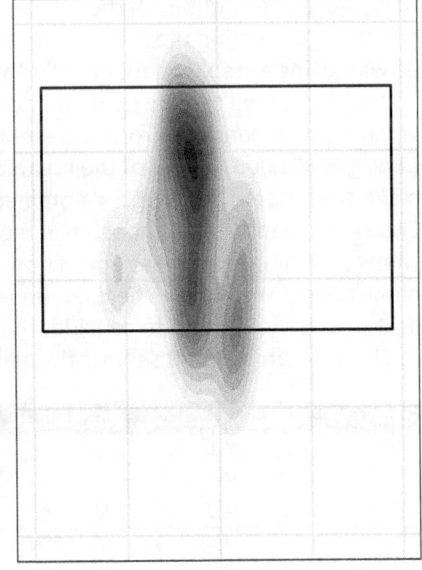

Shin-Soo Choo LF

Born: 07/13/82 Age: 38 Bats: L Throws: L
Height: 5'11" Weight: 205 Origin: International Free Agent, 2000

YEAR	TEAM	LVL	AGE	PA	R	2B	3B	HR	RBI	BB	K	SB	CS	AVG/OBP/SLG
2018	TEX	MLB	35	665	83	30	1	21	62	92	156	6	1	.264/.377/.434
2019	TEX	MLB	36	660	93	31	2	24	61	78	165	15	1	.265/.371/.455
2020	TEX	MLB	37	127	13	3	0	5	15	13	33	6	2	.236/.323/.400
2021 FS	TEX	MLB	38	600	69	24	1	19	69	69	166	10	4	.235/.342/.398
2021 DC	TEX	MLB	38	425	49	17	0	13	49	49	118	7	3	.235/.342/.398

Comparables: Jeromy Burnitz, Jayson Werth, Matt Stairs

 When the Rangers dished out $130 million to Choo seven years ago, they probably envisioned something different than what they received. They likely pictured elite plate discipline, with a rare combination of power and speed, not to mention a cannon arm from right field, all of which he delievered, at least in spurts. Injuries slowed Choo down on the bases, but he still worked a bunch of walks, and was even named an All-Star for the first time in 2018, in his age-35 season. It's possible to frame his tenure in Texas as a disappointment, but doing so would severely diminish the rest of what Choo brings to the table. There are plenty of guys within the Rangers organization that look up to Choo. Realizing he was losing a step, and that Leody Taveras was the lead-off hitter of the future, Choo volunteered to slide down the order and provide mentorship to the rookie. When a global pandemic rocked baseball (and pretty much everything else), Choo gave $1,000 to each of the organization's 190 minor leaguers struggling to make ends meet. The Rangers' nominee for the 2020 Roberto Clemente Award, Choo has meant a lot to the team in more than just on-field contribution. He wraps up that mega deal as South Korea's all-time leader in MLB homers, his 218 home runs more than the field combined. With questions swirling about Choo's next step, it's important to consider the totality of his contributions, and to celebrate a career spent serving the game.

YEAR	TEAM	LVL	AGE	PA	DRC+	BABIP	BRR	FRAA	WARP
2018	TEX	MLB	35	665	116	.330	-0.9	RF(34): -2.0, LF(26): -0.6	2.2
2019	TEX	MLB	36	660	112	.333	-0.2	RF(42): -4.1, LF(40): -0.4	2.0
2020	TEX	MLB	37	127	89	.284	0.8	LF(16): 1.1, RF(3): 0.7	0.2
2021 FS	TEX	MLB	38	600	104	.312	0.0	RF -2, LF 1	1.7
2021 DC	TEX	MLB	38	425	104	.312	0.0	RF -1, LF 1	1.2

Shin-Soo Choo, continued

Batted Ball Distribution

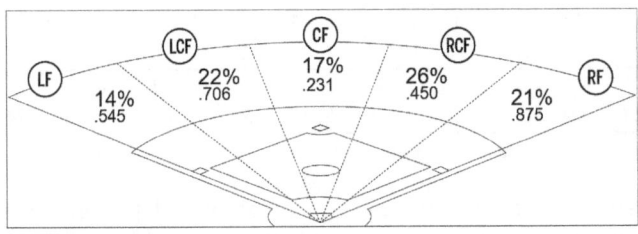

Strike Zone vs LHP   Strike Zone vs RHP

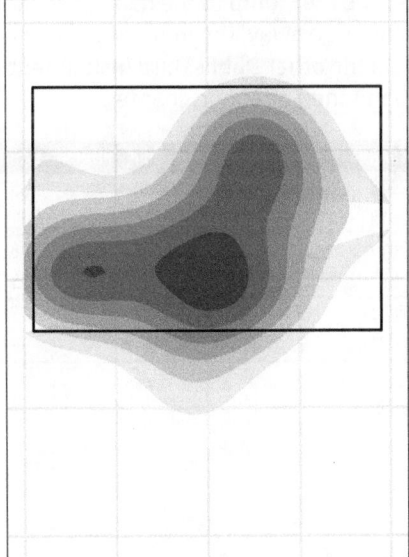

David Dahl LF

Born: 04/01/94 Age: 27 Bats: L Throws: R
Height: 6'2" Weight: 197 Origin: Round 1, 2012 Draft (#10 overall)

YEAR	TEAM	LVL	AGE	PA	R	2B	3B	HR	RBI	BB	K	SB	CS	AVG/OBP/SLG
2018	ABQ	AAA	24	78	7	7	0	2	9	1	19	1	0	.286/.295/.455
2018	COL	MLB	24	271	31	11	3	16	48	19	68	5	3	.273/.325/.534
2019	COL	MLB	25	413	67	28	5	15	61	28	110	4	4	.302/.353/.524
2020	COL	MLB	26	99	9	2	2	0	9	4	28	1	0	.183/.222/.247
2021 FS	TEX	MLB	27	600	71	26	6	22	66	36	170	8	3	.248/.299/.435
2021 DC	TEX	MLB	27	483	57	21	5	17	53	29	137	6	3	.248/.299/.435

Comparables: Al Martin, Trey Mancini, Corey Dickerson

    This is the first time a Dahl followed up a breakthrough performance with such a disappointment since *Charlie and the Great Glass Elevator*. Soreness wiped out all instances of his power, and his 2020 ranks among the most deficient seasons in Rockies history. (By OPS, minimum 50 PAs, it was sixth-worst). Despite that, it was a minor surprise that the Rockies non-tendered him; the Rangers quickly snatched him up hoping for a rebound. The more you ascribe the slump to the bad back, and the more likely you are to think back injuries go away, the more hopeful you become that he'll be way more effective than the other Dahl's third installment, *Charlie and the White House*, which was abandoned after one chapter.

YEAR	TEAM	LVL	AGE	PA	DRC+	BABIP	BRR	FRAA	WARP
2018	ABQ	AAA	24	78	85	.357	-0.6	CF(6): 0.4, RF(6): 0.2, LF(5): 1.7	0.1
2018	COL	MLB	24	271	112	.311	-1.3	LF(34): 2.9, RF(30): -1.4, CF(8): -0.4	1.1
2019	COL	MLB	25	413	103	.386	2.1	CF(40): 1.3, LF(39): 0.2, RF(24): -4.7	1.3
2020	COL	MLB	26	99	67	.258	0.7	CF(17): 0.5, LF(4): -0.7, RF(2): 0.1	-0.2
2021 FS	TEX	MLB	27	600	93	.321	0.8	LF 2, CF 0	1.3
2021 DC	TEX	MLB	27	483	93	.321	0.7	LF 1, CF 0	1.1

David Dahl, continued

Batted Ball Distribution

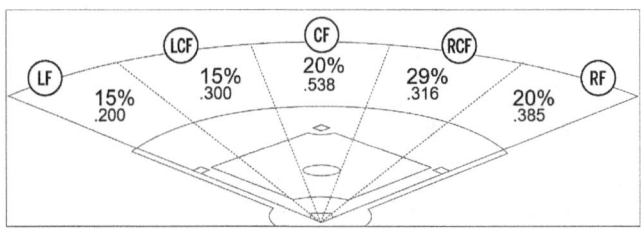

Strike Zone vs LHP   **Strike Zone vs RHP**

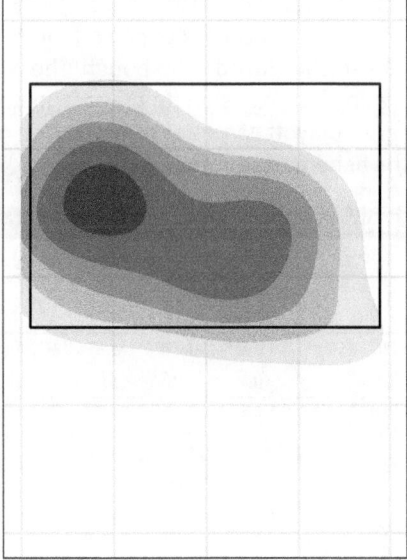

Khris Davis LF

Born: 12/21/87   Age: 33   Bats: R   Throws: R
Height: 5'11"   Weight: 205   Origin: Round 7, 2009 Draft (#226 overall)

YEAR	TEAM	LVL	AGE	PA	R	2B	3B	HR	RBI	BB	K	SB	CS	AVG/OBP/SLG
2018	OAK	MLB	30	654	98	28	1	48	123	59	175	0	0	.247/.326/.549
2019	OAK	MLB	31	533	61	11	0	23	73	47	146	0	0	.220/.293/.387
2020	OAK	MLB	32	99	9	5	0	2	10	10	26	0	0	.200/.303/.329
2021 FS	TEX	MLB	33	600	70	24	1	29	76	57	181	1	1	.227/.313/.439
2021 DC	TEX	MLB	33	325	38	13	0	15	41	31	98	0	1	.227/.313/.439

Comparables: Justin Upton, Geoff Jenkins, Marcus Thames

No one was ever quite sure what to make of Davis, even when he was hitting .247 annually and averaging 40 home runs between 2015 and 2018. Come 2019, right on the heels of an extension with the highest average annual value in A's history, the Khrush era suddenly appeared over. On the surface 2020 was only a confirmation Davis had gone off a steep cliff, with another sub-.700 OPS losing him playing time down the stretch. He did rebound to a .894 OPS in 32 September plate appearances, but the sample size speaks for itself: If you're going to believe in Davis in his age-33 season you're doing so on sentiment. Hoping for sentiment to pay off for the A's is a fool's errand, but Davis is the player who stayed, who bought the whole team Nintendo Switches upon signing his extension (to play Mario Kart on road trips), who got starts in six of seven playoff games after two torpid regular seasons; if anyone on the A's gets the benefit of sentiment, it's him.

YEAR	TEAM	LVL	AGE	PA	DRC+	BABIP	BRR	FRAA	WARP
2018	OAK	MLB	30	654	138	.261	-4.6	LF(11): -1.9	3.4
2019	OAK	MLB	31	533	91	.264	-1.6	LF(4): -0.3	0.1
2020	OAK	MLB	32	99	89	.259	-0.2		0.0
2021 FS	TEX	MLB	33	600	102	.287	-0.8	LF 0	1.6
2021 DC	TEX	MLB	33	325	102	.287	-0.5		0.6

Khris Davis, continued

Batted Ball Distribution

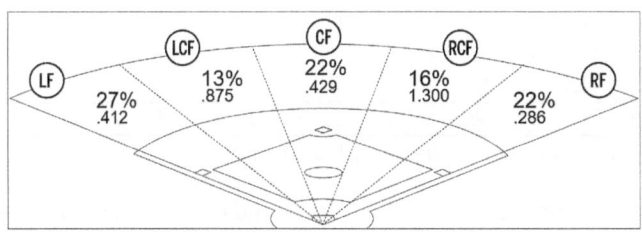

Strike Zone vs LHP   Strike Zone vs RHP

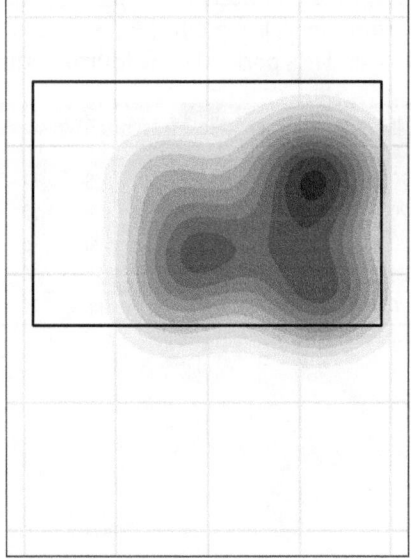

Delino DeShields CF

Born: 08/16/92   Age: 28   Bats: R   Throws: R
Height: 5'9"   Weight: 190   Origin: Round 1, 2010 Draft (#8 overall)

YEAR	TEAM	LVL	AGE	PA	R	2B	3B	HR	RBI	BB	K	SB	CS	AVG/OBP/SLG
2018	FRI	AA	25	26	2	0	0	0	0	8	2	2	2	.278/.500/.278
2018	TEX	MLB	25	393	52	14	1	2	22	43	83	20	4	.216/.310/.281
2019	NAS	AAA	26	75	10	3	0	3	11	8	17	8	0	.258/.338/.439
2019	TEX	MLB	26	408	42	15	4	4	32	38	100	24	6	.249/.325/.347
2020	CLE	MLB	27	120	10	3	2	0	7	9	29	3	2	.252/.310/.318
2021 FS	TEX	MLB	28	600	56	21	2	9	53	63	154	29	9	.224/.312/.325

Comparables: Jermaine Allensworth, Carroll Hardy, Ryan Christenson

What could say more about the 2020 Cleveland outfield than the light-hitting DeShields *raising* the unit's collective OPS? How about this: at .575, the Cleveland outfield had the worst OPS in MLB history. There's an element of small-sample variance to that tidbit, best evidenced by the 2020 Pirates ranking second-worst. Nonetheless, playing on the grass for Cleveland meant hitting like a player from the Dead Ball Era. We would say 'hitting like a Cleveland Spider', except the infamous 1899 Spiders actually put up a better offensive performance. DeShields himself maintained his career offensive level, by the way, and is a perfectly fine fourth outfielder with speed and good defense.

YEAR	TEAM	LVL	AGE	PA	DRC+	BABIP	BRR	FRAA	WARP
2018	FRI	AA	25	26	171	.312	-0.9	CF(5): -0.5	0.1
2018	TEX	MLB	25	393	72	.280	3.4	CF(102): 10.3	1.5
2019	NAS	AAA	26	75	92	.304	1.6	CF(13): 1.1, LF(1): 0.8	0.5
2019	TEX	MLB	26	408	76	.333	4.9	CF(112): 6.9	1.4
2020	CLE	MLB	27	120	66	.346	-0.8	CF(35): 4.6	0.2
2021 FS	TEX	MLB	28	600	79	.298	2.1	CF 5, LF 0	1.0

Delino DeShields, continued

Batted Ball Distribution

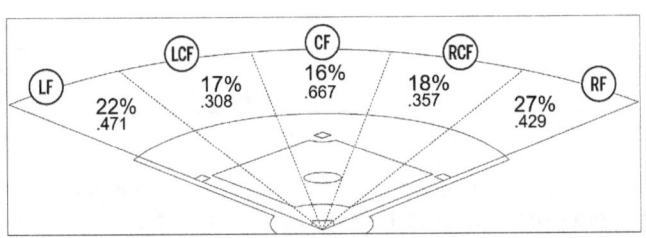

Strike Zone vs LHP   Strike Zone vs RHP

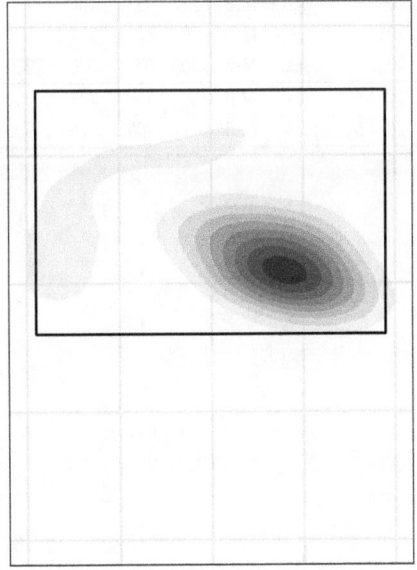

Derek Dietrich 2B

Born: 07/18/89 Age: 31 Bats: L Throws: R
Height: 6'2" Weight: 205 Origin: Round 2, 2010 Draft (#79 overall)

YEAR	TEAM	LVL	AGE	PA	R	2B	3B	HR	RBI	BB	K	SB	CS	AVG/OBP/SLG
2018	MIA	MLB	28	551	72	26	2	16	45	29	140	2	0	.265/.330/.421
2019	CIN	MLB	29	306	41	8	2	19	43	28	74	1	1	.187/.328/.462
2020	TEX	MLB	30	75	9	1	0	5	8	9	21	1	1	.197/.347/.459
2021 FS	TEX	MLB	31	600	76	25	3	25	80	48	160	2	1	.239/.348/.449
2021 DC	TEX	MLB	31	300	38	12	1	12	40	24	80	0	1	.239/.348/.449

Comparables: Kelly Johnson, Rickie Weeks Jr., Junior Spivey

Dietrich looks like a man who practices transcendental meditation in an igloo formed out of old Axe Spray cans. He's also the model of a modern pinch hitter, and the antonym of the Dave Hansens and Lenny Harrises of yesteryear. It seems strange to think, but he could hang around for years doing this; few can make their inconsistency so consistently productive.

YEAR	TEAM	LVL	AGE	PA	DRC+	BABIP	BRR	FRAA	WARP
2018	MIA	MLB	28	551	100	.336	1.7	LF(97): -8.4, 1B(33): -1.9, 2B(4): -0.1	0.4
2019	CIN	MLB	29	306	112	.176	1.5	2B(58): -3.1, 1B(21): -0.7, LF(16): -1.1	1.1
2020	TEX	MLB	30	75	99	.200	-0.1	1B(6): -0.5, 2B(3): -0.5, 3B(3): 0.1	0.0
2021 FS	TEX	MLB	31	600	116	.300	-0.4	LF -2, 1B 0	2.3
2021 DC	TEX	MLB	31	300	116	.300	-0.2	LF -1, 1B 0	1.2

Derek Dietrich, continued

Batted Ball Distribution

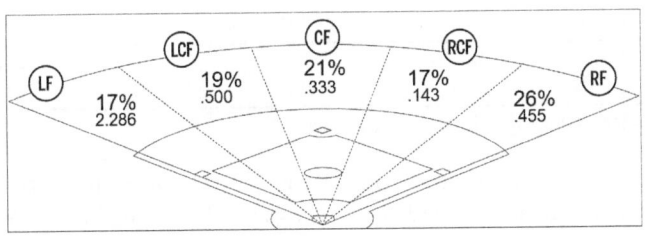

Strike Zone vs LHP **Strike Zone vs RHP**

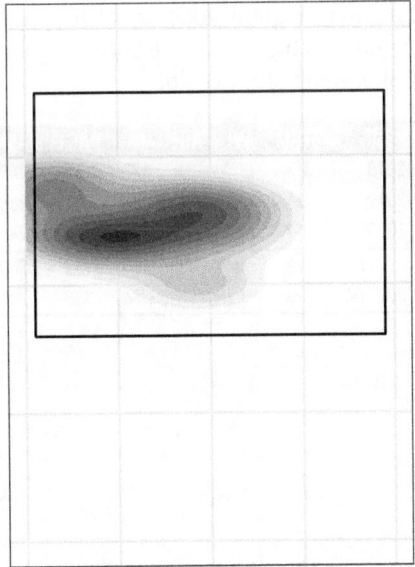

Joey Gallo CF

Born: 11/19/93 Age: 27 Bats: L Throws: R
Height: 6'5" Weight: 250 Origin: Round 1, 2012 Draft (#39 overall)

YEAR	TEAM	LVL	AGE	PA	R	2B	3B	HR	RBI	BB	K	SB	CS	AVG/OBP/SLG
2018	TEX	MLB	24	577	82	24	1	40	92	74	207	3	4	.206/.312/.498
2019	TEX	MLB	25	297	54	15	1	22	49	52	114	4	2	.253/.389/.598
2020	TEX	MLB	26	226	23	8	0	10	26	29	79	2	0	.181/.301/.378
2021 FS	TEX	MLB	27	600	81	23	2	35	83	86	228	5	2	.211/.335/.473
2021 DC	TEX	MLB	27	576	78	22	2	33	79	83	219	5	2	.211/.335/.473

Comparables: Adam Dunn, Kyle Schwarber, Rob Deer

Can you name the dude with 80 power, Hits 'em a hundred miles an hour Joey Gallo! Joey Gallo! (whip crack) Well, he swings real hard, puts the hammer down He's the only true outcome endorsed by a clown Joey Gallo! Joey Gallo!

[ANNOUNCER VOICE] Globe Life Field has ruled it unsafe to sit in the bleachers during Joey Gallo BP.

Cannon for an arm and a stealthy quick stride, Patrols the outfield with a long-legged glide. Joey Gallo! Joey Gallo! (Yah!) Oblique, hamate, wrist—he gets injured each year, It's the only thing stopping a successful career. He's Joey Gallo, woah! Joey Gallo!

YEAR	TEAM	LVL	AGE	PA	DRC+	BABIP	BRR	FRAA	WARP
2018	TEX	MLB	24	577	115	.249	1.9	LF(85): -6.3, 1B(35): 3.1, RF(16): 3.4	2.7
2019	TEX	MLB	25	297	128	.368	1.7	CF(30): 0.0, LF(34). 4.1	2.6
2020	TEX	MLB	26	226	84	.240	1.6	RF(53): 5.3, CF(1): -0.0	0.8
2021 FS	TEX	MLB	27	600	113	.300	-0.1	RF 10, 1B 0	3.5
2021 DC	TEX	MLB	27	576	113	.300	-0.1	RF 9	3.1

Joey Gallo, continued

Batted Ball Distribution

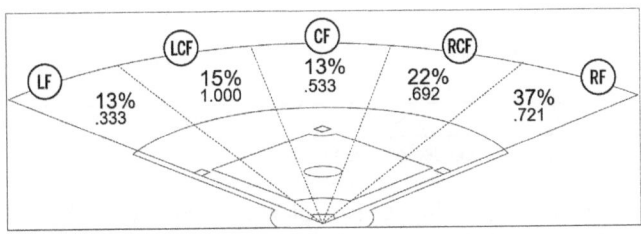

Strike Zone vs LHP   Strike Zone vs RHP

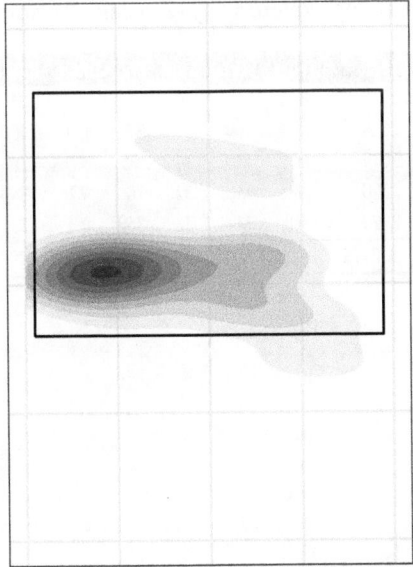

Texas Rangers 2021

Brock Holt 2B
Born: 06/11/88 Age: 33 Bats: L Throws: R
Height: 5'10" Weight: 180 Origin: Round 9, 2009 Draft (#265 overall)

YEAR	TEAM	LVL	AGE	PA	R	2B	3B	HR	RBI	BB	K	SB	CS	AVG/OBP/SLG
2018	BOS	MLB	30	367	41	18	2	7	46	37	73	7	7	.277/.362/.411
2019	WOR	AAA	31	37	7	2	0	1	3	8	12	1	0	.250/.432/.429
2019	BOS	MLB	31	295	38	14	2	3	31	28	57	1	0	.297/.369/.402
2020	WAS	MLB	32	70	11	6	0	0	4	5	15	1	0	.262/.314/.354
2020	MIL	MLB	32	36	1	0	0	0	1	4	9	0	0	.100/.222/.100
2021 FS	TEX	MLB	33	600	58	25	1	11	57	59	139	8	4	.234/.322/.350

Comparables: Dick Green, Randy Velarde, Tony Graffanino

    Holt is the second do-it-all late-season pickup to experience the Nationals utilityman bump. In 2019, Asdrúbal Cabrera went from meh to machine after being DFA by the Rangers. Holt was similarly flailing, coming off a 3-for-30 stretch with Milwaukee, when he joined the Nats as part of their attempts to patchwork one (1) competent infielder from a scrapheap of designated hitters. Holt's offense returned, albeit over a small sample, and he'll likely continue as a fielding skeleton key who can also sometimes make good contact.

YEAR	TEAM	LVL	AGE	PA	DRC+	BABIP	BRR	FRAA	WARP
2018	BOS	MLB	30	367	101	.337	-1.9	2B(56): -5.3, SS(23): -2.0, RF(11): -0.7	0.1
2019	WOR	AAA	31	37	107	.400	0.0	SS(3): 1.1, 2B(2): -0.3	0.2
2019	BOS	MLB	31	295	97	.365	-1.1	2B(60): 3.7, 1B(11): 1.7, SS(6): 0.6	1.3
2020	WAS	MLB	32	70	77	.340	1.3	LF(6): -0.4, 3B(5): 0.0, 1B(4): 0.5	0.0
2020	MIL	MLB	32	36	77	.136	0.1	3B(13): -0.5, LF(3): 0.2, RF(1): -0.1	0.0
2021 FS	TEX	MLB	33	600	87	.299	-0.1	2B 0, SS 1	0.6

Brock Holt, continued

Batted Ball Distribution

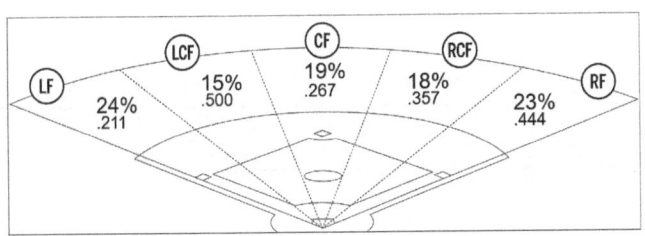

Strike Zone vs LHP   Strike Zone vs RHP

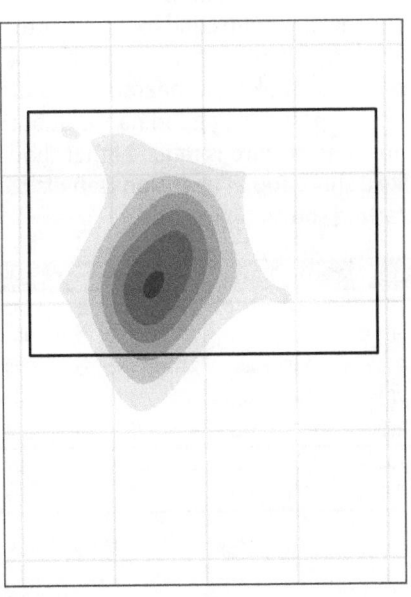

Type	Frequency	Velocity	H Movement	V Movement
● Fastball	81.3%	75 [44]	-6.5 [101]	-26.1 [69]
▲ Changeup	6.3%	56.4 [-12]	-1.4 [155]	-70.5 [-18]

Texas Rangers 2021

Isiah Kiner-Falefa 3B
Born: 03/23/95 Age: 26 Bats: R Throws: R
Height: 5'11" Weight: 190 Origin: Round 4, 2013 Draft (#130 overall)

YEAR	TEAM	LVL	AGE	PA	R	2B	3B	HR	RBI	BB	K	SB	CS	AVG/OBP/SLG
2018	TEX	MLB	23	396	43	18	2	4	34	28	62	7	5	.261/.325/.357
2019	FRI	AA	24	71	7	4	0	2	11	8	9	1	0	.283/.380/.450
2019	NAS	AAA	24	37	3	3	0	0	2	1	6	1	0	.147/.216/.235
2019	TEX	MLB	24	222	23	12	1	1	21	14	49	3	0	.238/.299/.322
2020	TEX	MLB	25	228	28	4	3	3	10	14	32	8	5	.280/.329/.370
2021 FS	TEX	MLB	26	600	66	26	2	8	57	43	103	5	2	.259/.328/.366
2021 DC	TEX	MLB	26	556	61	24	2	8	52	40	96	5	2	.259/.328/.366

Comparables: Tim Hulett, Aaron Boone, Frank Kostro

The Rangers moved into a new stadium this year. The concept art was undoubtedly beautiful, but the finished product somewhat less so, unless you're hoping for a ballpark more reminiscent of a Home Depot. One Ranger that did enjoy his new digs, however, was Kiner-Falefa, who led the team in hitting at home, coming up just shy of .300 in 28 games. Over the last couple of seasons, the team tried to fit him into a jack-of-all-trades, master of none role, including a spell as the backup backstop. This year Kiner-Falefa shed the tools of ignorance, making appearances exclusively splitting time at third base and shortstop, showing good hands at both spots. The problem is that the offensive threshold at third is much higher than it is behind the dish, and Kiner-Falefa hits like a shortstop at best. Jon Daniels considered this, and made him their starting shortstop for 2021.

YEAR	TEAM	LVL	AGE	PA	DRC+	BABIP	BRR	FRAA	WARP
2018	TEX	MLB	23	396	85	.306	-0.6	3B(46): 3.4, C(35): -10.1, 2B(20): -0.2	0.1
2019	FRI	AA	24	71	152	.300	-0.1	C(9): -0.7, 3B(4): 1.5, SS(1): -0.1	0.7
2019	NAS	AAA	24	37	33	.179	-0.7	SS(4): 0.2, C(2): 0.0	-0.2
2019	TEX	MLB	24	222	71	.307	1.8	C(38): -11.0, 3B(25): 1.7	-0.5
2020	TEX	MLB	25	228	82	.316	1.2	3B(46): -0.2, SS(15): 0.7	0.2
2021 FS	TEX	MLB	26	600	92	.309	-0.2	SS 1, 3B 1	0.9
2021 DC	TEX	MLB	26	556	92	.309	-0.2	SS 1, 3B 1	1.1

Isiah Kiner-Falefa, continued

Batted Ball Distribution

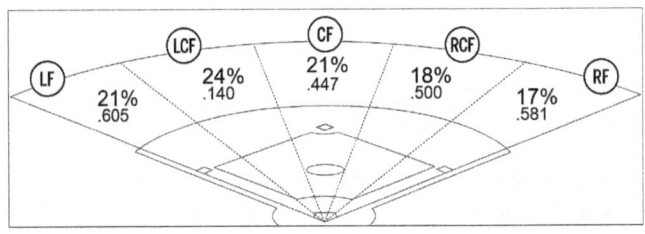

Strike Zone vs LHP   Strike Zone vs RHP

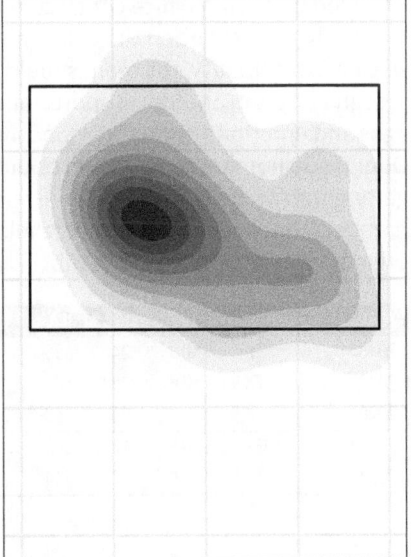

Rougned Odor 2B

Born: 02/03/94   Age: 27   Bats: L   Throws: R
Height: 5'11"   Weight: 200   Origin: International Free Agent, 2011

YEAR	TEAM	LVL	AGE	PA	R	2B	3B	HR	RBI	BB	K	SB	CS	AVG/OBP/SLG
2018	TEX	MLB	24	535	76	23	2	18	63	43	127	12	12	.253/.326/.424
2019	TEX	MLB	25	581	77	30	1	30	93	52	178	11	9	.205/.283/.439
2020	TEX	MLB	26	148	15	4	0	10	30	7	47	0	1	.167/.209/.413
2021 FS	TEX	MLB	27	600	69	25	2	29	76	39	167	13	6	.224/.288/.438
2021 DC	TEX	MLB	27	264	30	11	1	13	33	17	73	5	3	.224/.288/.438

Comparables: Danny Espinosa, Derek Dietrich, Scooter Gennett

In 2017, Odor played in a major league-leading 162 games. In 2018, he led the American League in times caught stealing. In 2019, he struck out 178 times, which, you guess it, paced the AL. In 2020, Odor was the only guy in the league to take off his skate and try to stab a guy. Ok, fine, one of those is made up. It has been a strange career for Odor, who has run the gamut of contact-oriented prospect, emerging power hitter, and a dude that pretty much can't hit at all—all before the age of 27. After breaking through in 2016, the Rangers provided Odor with a nice contract extension, complete with two horses (seriously). He rewarded the club with a line of .215/.279/.416 over the next four seasons. In actuality, the team should have held its horses. Sunk costs aren't recognized often enough in sports, and it makes sense. In a landscape where egos and emotions run high, nobody wants to admit to a costly mistake. Could Odor hit 30 homers again? Sure! Could he steal double-digit bases while also getting thrown out a bunch? Almost definitely! Would those be mostly empty numbers that likely impede the development of the next guy up in the organization? Therein lies the rub.

YEAR	TEAM	LVL	AGE	PA	DRC+	BABIP	BRR	FRAA	WARP
2018	TEX	MLB	24	535	97	.305	1.0	2B(127): 7.5	2.4
2019	TEX	MLB	25	581	87	.244	-2.8	2B(137): -12.8	-0.6
2020	TEX	MLB	26	148	69	.157	0.3	2B(37): 1.0	0.0
2021 FS	TEX	MLB	27	600	91	.267	1.0	2B 0	1.2
2021 DC	TEX	MLB	27	264	91	.267	0.5	2B 0, 3B 0	0.4

Rougned Odor, continued

Batted Ball Distribution

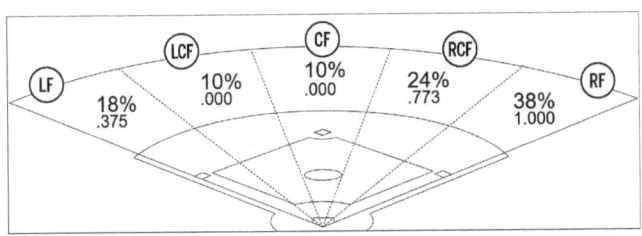

Strike Zone vs LHP   Strike Zone vs RHP

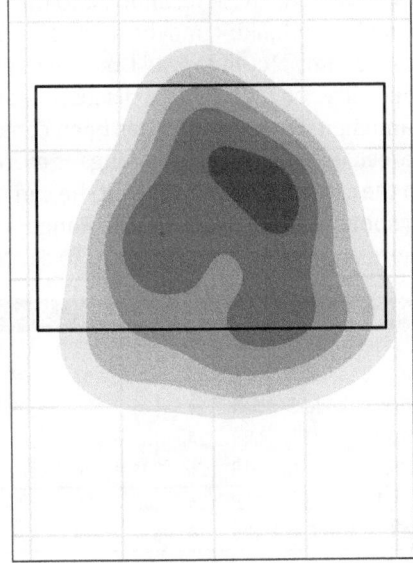

Nick Solak OF

Born: 01/11/95   Age: 26   Bats: R   Throws: R
Height: 5'11"   Weight: 185   Origin: Round 2, 2016 Draft (#62 overall)

YEAR	TEAM	LVL	AGE	PA	R	2B	3B	HR	RBI	BB	K	SB	CS	AVG/OBP/SLG
2018	MTG	AA	23	565	91	17	3	19	76	68	112	21	6	.282/.384/.450
2019	DUR	AAA	24	349	56	13	1	17	47	39	80	3	2	.266/.353/.485
2019	NAS	AAA	24	128	23	6	0	10	27	6	25	2	0	.347/.386/.653
2019	TEX	MLB	24	135	19	6	1	5	17	15	29	2	0	.293/.393/.491
2020	TEX	MLB	25	233	27	10	0	2	23	18	42	7	1	.268/.326/.344
2021 FS	TEX	MLB	26	600	77	29	2	20	72	52	129	4	2	.278/.353/.453
2021 DC	TEX	MLB	26	584	75	29	2	19	70	50	126	3	2	.278/.353/.453

Comparables: Ozzie Timmons, Kevin Mench, Alex Gordon

    We could talk about Solak's college team, the Louisville Cardinals, chock full of future big leaguers (and big-league hopefuls) like Will Smith, Brendan McKay, and Corey Ray. However, that team was bounced prematurely in the postseason, thanks to a date with UC Santa Barbara and future-Cy Young award winner Shane Bieber. We could check in with Solak's other alma mater, Naperville North High School, and maybe tie in some cute references to fellow alum Bob Odenkirk, maybe a Better Call Saul nod, hoping Solak can transform from Jimmy McGill to Saul Goodman. Without any standout options, that pretty much just leaves us with a discussion of Solak's slightly underwhelming rookie campaign. For a guy that has been considered "bat-only" for most of his pro career, you're probably looking for more than 12 extra base hits in over 200 trips to the plate. Still, Solak can hit, he can run, and he can fake defense in a couple of spots. He'll be useful for the Rangers moving forward (with the possibility for more), no matter how you want to contextualize it.

YEAR	TEAM	LVL	AGE	PA	DRC+	BABIP	BRR	FRAA	WARP
2018	MTG	AA	23	565	138	.330	-0.5	2B(60): -6.9, LF(40): -3.3, CF(18): 0.8	1.7
2019	DUR	AAA	24	349	107	.303	-3.6	2B(61): -7.5, LF(17): 0.4, CF(2): -0.2	0.3
2019	NAS	AAA	24	128	134	.369	0.7	2B(22): 0.4, RF(4): 0.3, LF(3): 0.1	1.0
2019	TEX	MLB	24	135	109	.354	1.3	3B(11): -0.1, 2B(5): -0.7	0.6
2020	TEX	MLB	25	233	88	.320	2.5	LF(29): -0.6, 2B(17): -1.7, CF(13): 0.0	0.3
2021 FS	TEX	MLB	26	600	119	.337	-0.4	2B -3, LF 0	2.8
2021 DC	TEX	MLB	26	584	119	.337	-0.4	2B -3, LF 0	2.8

Nick Solak, continued

Batted Ball Distribution

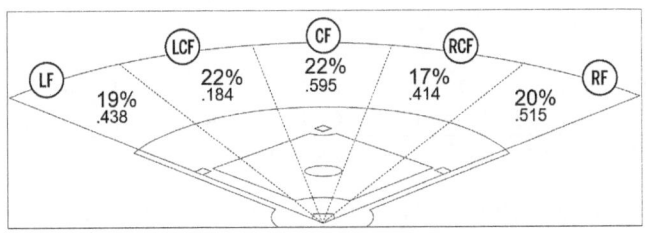

Strike Zone vs LHP   **Strike Zone vs RHP**

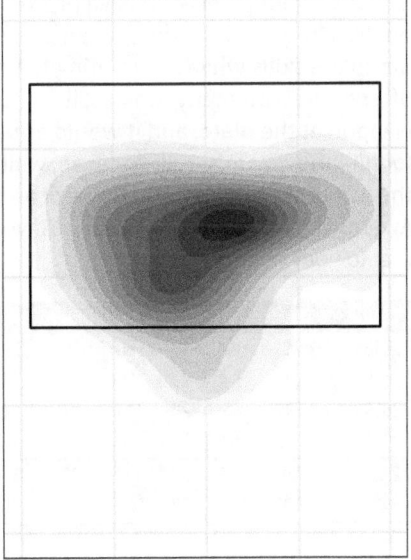

Leody Taveras CF

Born: 09/08/98   Age: 22   Bats: S   Throws: R
Height: 6'2"   Weight: 195   Origin: International Free Agent, 2015

YEAR	TEAM	LVL	AGE	PA	R	2B	3B	HR	RBI	BB	K	SB	CS	AVG/OBP/SLG
2018	DE	HI-A	19	580	65	16	7	5	48	51	96	19	11	.246/.312/.332
2019	DE	HI-A	20	290	44	7	4	2	25	31	62	21	5	.294/.368/.376
2019	FRI	AA	20	293	32	12	4	3	31	23	60	11	8	.265/.320/.375
2020	TEX	MLB	21	134	20	6	1	4	6	14	43	8	0	.227/.308/.395
2021 FS	TEX	MLB	22	600	68	25	4	10	46	46	172	11	6	.224/.287/.345
2021 DC	TEX	MLB	22	570	64	24	4	10	44	44	163	10	6	.224/.287/.345

Comparables: Derrick Robinson, Luis Alexander Basabe, Xavier Avery

    Former MacArthur Fellow and Pulitzer Prize winning poet Mark Strand once wrote that "the future is always beginning now." It's an idea that is profound enough in its simplicity, and five years after signing with the Rangers as a 16-year-old out of the Dominican Republic, it's an idea that can finally apply to Taveras. After spending years tabbed as the center fielder of the future in Arlington, while lingering amid top-100 lists, Taveras made his big-league debut in 2020. Although his offensive prowess didn't set the world ablaze, he did strike out less frequently as the season progressed, flashing newly minted plate discipline skills while acclimating to battling major-league hurlers from the lead-off spot. As with many rookies, it will be a process for Taveras to develop into a weapon at the plate, and it would appear as though it will be on-the-job training for him moving forward, because, well, the future is now for the center fielder of the future. As another great American poet and two-time iHeartRadio Music Award winner, Pitbull, once said, "If you continue to work hard, let that be the fuel to your fire."

YEAR	TEAM	LVL	AGE	PA	DRC+	BABIP	BRR	FRAA	WARP
2018	DE	HI-A	19	580	90	.292	0.3	CF(123): 7.0, RF(3): 0.0	0.8
2019	DE	HI-A	20	290	123	.378	-0.4	CF(34): -0.6, RF(23): 4.0, LF(7): -0.7	1.7
2019	FRI	AA	20	293	97	.327	0.5	CF(65): 8.1	1.8
2020	TEX	MLB	21	134	84	.319	1.1	CF(33): 0.9	0.4
2021 FS	TEX	MLB	22	600	70	.308	1.1	CF 9, LF 0	0.6
2021 DC	TEX	MLB	22	570	70	.308	1.0	CF 9	0.6

Leody Taveras, continued

Batted Ball Distribution

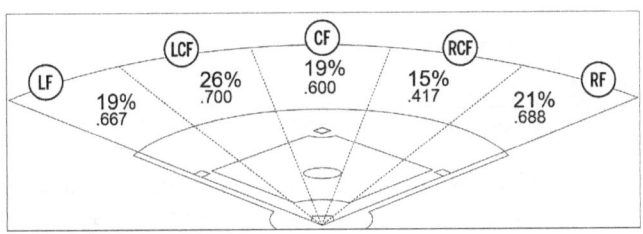

Strike Zone vs LHP   **Strike Zone vs RHP**

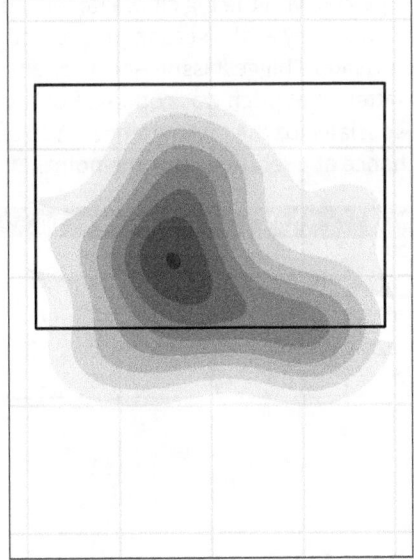

Anderson Tejeda SS

Born: 05/01/98   Age: 23   Bats: S   Throws: R
Height: 6'0"   Weight: 200   Origin: International Free Agent, 2014

YEAR	TEAM	LVL	AGE	PA	R	2B	3B	HR	RBI	BB	K	SB	CS	AVG/OBP/SLG
2018	DE	HI-A	20	522	76	17	5	19	74	49	142	11	4	.259/.331/.439
2019	DE	HI-A	21	181	22	10	1	4	24	17	58	9	4	.234/.315/.386
2020	TEX	MLB	22	77	7	4	1	3	8	2	30	4	1	.253/.273/.453
2021 FS	TEX	MLB	23	600	61	25	5	18	65	34	229	4	3	.214/.264/.374
2021 DC	TEX	MLB	23	248	25	10	2	7	26	14	94	2	1	.214/.264/.374

Comparables: Junior Lake, Gleyber Torres, Marcus Semien

Hitting is really hard. In most cases it combines the mental acuity and strategy of a master-level chess match with the physical prowess necessary to use a piece of lumber to smack a cork wound in yarn and cowhide, all with a reaction time of less than half a second. Take Tejeda, for instance. The 22-year-old was one of many rookies to debut without experience above High-A this season, and his first bout with big-league pitching went about as expected. Initially, Tejeda saw a bunch of fastballs, and he was ready, socking a pair of dingers in his first 11 games with the big club. Pitchers adjusted, chucking more breaking balls Tejeda's way as the season progressed, and the rookie struggled, shedding light on Tejada's biggest issue—his propensity for succumbing to the strikeout, no matter what pitch was coming. But there's one nice thing about hitting, especially for the inexperienced: You get so many tries. Tejeda will get his chance at a rebuttal, at some point.

YEAR	TEAM	LVL	AGE	PA	DRC+	BABIP	BRR	FRAA	WARP
2018	DE	HI-A	20	522	119	.330	3.0	SS(105): 2.9, 2B(12): 1.6	2.9
2019	DE	HI-A	21	181	83	.333	1.3	SS(39): 2.4	0.8
2020	TEX	MLB	22	77	76	.381	0.1	SS(18): -0.2, 2B(4): -0.1	0.0
2021 FS	TEX	MLB	23	600	69	.326	0.5	SS 1, 2B 2	-0.3
2021 DC	TEX	MLB	23	248	69	.326	0.2	SS 0, 2B 1	-0.1

Anderson Tejeda, continued

Batted Ball Distribution

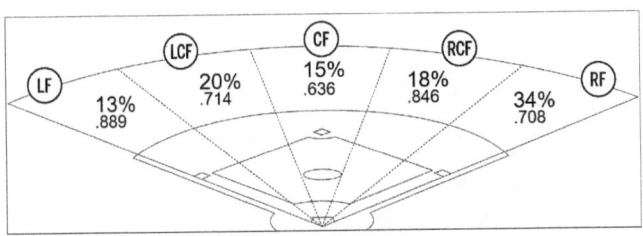

Strike Zone vs LHP   **Strike Zone vs RHP**

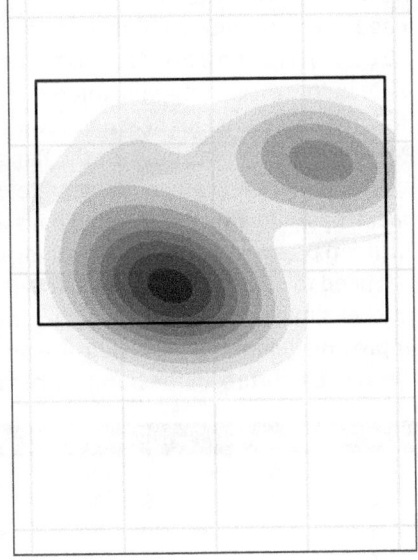

Jose Trevino C

Born: 11/28/92 Age: 28 Bats: R Throws: R
Height: 5'11" Weight: 210 Origin: Round 6, 2014 Draft (#186 overall)

YEAR	TEAM	LVL	AGE	PA	R	2B	3B	HR	RBI	BB	K	SB	CS	AVG/OBP/SLG
2018	FRI	AA	25	201	18	7	1	3	16	13	27	0	1	.234/.284/.332
2018	TEX	MLB	25	8	0	0	0	0	3	0	1	0	0	.250/.250/.250
2019	RAN	ROK	26	38	3	1	0	1	6	2	2	0	0	.167/.211/.278
2019	NAS	AAA	26	156	16	10	0	2	22	8	28	2	0	.226/.263/.336
2019	TEX	MLB	26	126	18	9	0	2	13	3	27	0	0	.258/.272/.383
2020	TEX	MLB	27	83	10	8	0	2	9	3	15	0	0	.250/.280/.434
2021 FS	TEX	MLB	28	600	58	27	1	13	61	27	117	0	1	.231/.271/.353
2021 DC	TEX	MLB	28	348	33	15	0	7	35	16	68	0	0	.231/.271/.353

Comparables: Josh Phegley, Todd Greene, Mark Parent

On offense, going from Jeff Mathis to pretty much anyone is akin to jumping from roller skates to a Tesla. While that might be too high of praise to heap on Trevino, the rookie took to major-league pitching with aplomb, hitting .291/.333/.473 in his first 60 trips to the plate before an errant swing injured his wrist and ended his season.

YEAR	TEAM	P. COUNT	FRM RUNS	BLK RUNS	THRW RUNS	TOT RUNS
2018	TEX	281	-0.2	-0.2		-0.4
2018	FRI	5465	6.0	0.5	0.6	7.1
2019	TEX	5134	0.8	0.0	0.0	0.8
2019	NAS	5718	7.3	0.2	0.0	7.4
2020	TEX	2650	1.8	0.0	0.1	1.8
2021	TEX	13228	5.7	-0.7	-0.5	4.4
2021	TEX	13228	5.7	-1.3	-0.5	3.9

Perhaps more importantly for the Rangers' plans, he acquitted himself just as nicely behind the plate, posting better defensive metrics than all but 13 other backstops, allowing zero passed balls and significantly improving his framing. With top prospect Sam Huff breathing down his neck, it's progress that Trevino will need to continue if he wants to keep getting first-team reps donning the catcher's mask. Even still, his high-contact approach–in addition to steadily improving defense–should help Trevino to keep getting chances for the foreseeable future, in the Rangers' organization or elsewhere.

YEAR	TEAM	LVL	AGE	PA	DRC+	BABIP	BRR	FRAA	WARP
2018	FRI	AA	25	201	76	.255	-0.8	C(38): 8.0	0.6
2018	TEX	MLB	25	8	82	.286		C(3): -0.5	0.0
2019	RAN	ROK	26	38		.152			
2019	NAS	AAA	26	156	45	.263	0.7	C(40): 6.4	0.5
2019	TEX	MLB	26	126	77	.312	-0.7	C(40): 0.5	0.3
2020	TEX	MLB	27	83	95	.279	0.7	C(21): -0.1, 1B(1): -0.0	0.4
2021 FS	TEX	MLB	28	600	68	.272	-1.0	C 6, 1B 0	0.4
2021 DC	TEX	MLB	28	348	68	.272	-0.6	C 4	0.4

Jose Trevino, continued

Batted Ball Distribution

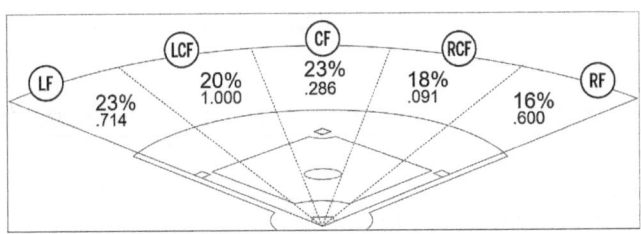

Strike Zone vs LHP   **Strike Zone vs RHP**

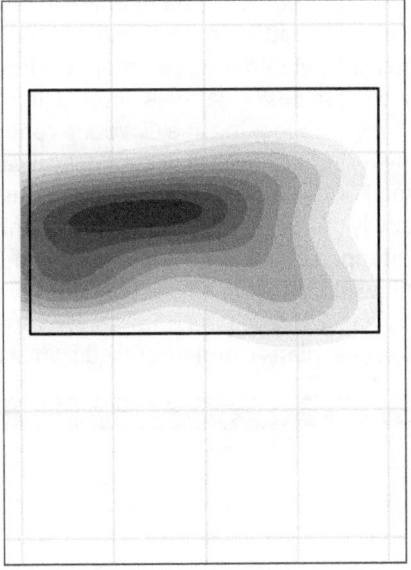

Kolby Allard LHP

Born: 08/13/97 Age: 23 Bats: L Throws: L
Height: 6'1" Weight: 195 Origin: Round 1, 2015 Draft (#14 overall)

YEAR	TEAM	LVL	AGE	W	L	SV	G	GS	IP	H	HR	BB/9	K/9	K	GB%	BABIP
2018	GWN	AAA	20	6	4	0	19	19	112^1	102	6	2.7	7.1	89	37.3%	.301
2018	ATL	MLB	20	1	1	0	3	1	8	19	3	4.5	3.4	3	33.3%	.457
2019	NAS	AAA	21	0	0	0	1	1	5	4	0	3.6	14.4	8	44.4%	.444
2019	GWN	AAA	21	7	5	0	20	20	110	119	15	2.9	8.0	98	49.2%	.334
2019	TEX	MLB	21	4	2	0	9	9	45^1	52	3	3.8	6.6	33	45.1%	.327
2020	TEX	MLB	22	0	6	0	11	8	33^2	31	4	5.3	8.6	32	34.3%	.284
2021 FS	TEX	MLB	23	9	9	0	26	26	150	155	24	3.6	7.6	126	40.8%	.300
2021 DC	TEX	MLB	23	5	5	0	22	16	76	78	12	3.6	7.6	64	40.8%	.300

Comparables: José Suarez, Julio Teheran, Taijuan Walker

    Allard's statline reflected the woes of the year at large. The lefty spent his sophomore season in Texas serving up a litany of free passes, posting one of the highest walk rates in baseball before ultimately finding his way to the bullpen for his final three appearances. Even so, if you peel off a Coors Field start that yielded six earned in three innings, followed up by another four in 2/3 of an inning in Seattle, you're looking at a much better bottom line. And why stop there? By eliminating two more back-to-back September starts against the A's and those pesky Mariners where Allard gave up 14 runs in 4 2/3 frames, well, now you're looking at a Cy Young candidate. Unfortunately, neither Allard nor the rest of us have those time-travel capabilities, so we're stuck with what we've got. For the southpaw, there's still time to turn things around. His changeup has slowly morphed into his best pitch, and with a usage rate under 13 percent, untapped efficiency is available. In addition, more than half of the baserunners allowed by Allard came around to score, a shocking number that should regress favorably. If it doesn't, though, it's very possible that Allard's presence in the Rangers' plans could be erased from existence.

YEAR	TEAM	LVL	AGE	WHIP	ERA	DRA-	WARP	MPH	FB%	WHF	CSP
2018	GWN	AAA	20	1.21	2.72	94	1.1				
2018	ATL	MLB	20	2.88	12.38	188	-0.3	90.9	62.7%	12.3%	
2019	NAS	AAA	21	1.20	0.00	47	0.2				
2019	GWN	AAA	21	1.41	4.17	93	2.3				
2019	TEX	MLB	21	1.57	4.96	123	-0.1	93.5	79.6%	19.0%	
2020	TEX	MLB	22	1.51	7.75	129	-0.2	92.8	77.2%	23.2%	
2021 FS	TEX	MLB	23	1.43	4.74	108	0.8	93.0	77.6%	20.9%	52.5%
2021 DC	TEX	MLB	23	1.43	4.74	108	0.4	93.0	77.6%	20.9%	52.5%

Kolby Allard, continued

Pitch Shape vs LHH   **Pitch Shape vs RHH**

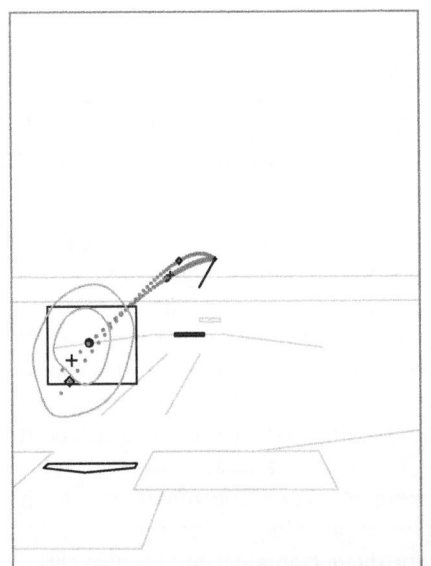 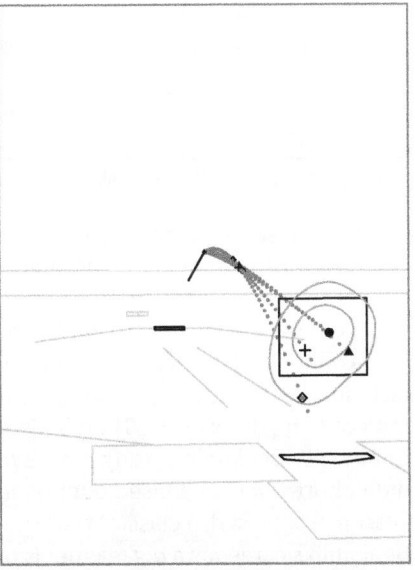

Type	Frequency	Velocity	H Movement	V Movement
● Fastball	46.5%	91.7 [97]	7.7 [95]	-14.6 [102]
+ Cutter	30.7%	86.9 [91]	-2.6 [104]	-26.1 [93]
▲ Changeup	12.6%	82.6 [90]	11.2 [103]	-25.1 [107]
◇ Curveball	10.2%	76.8 [93]	-4.7 [88]	-50.9 [94]

Wes Benjamin LHP

Born: 07/26/93   Age: 27   Bats: R   Throws: L
Height: 6'2"   Weight: 210   Origin: Round 5, 2014 Draft (#156 overall)

YEAR	TEAM	LVL	AGE	W	L	SV	G	GS	IP	H	HR	BB/9	K/9	K	GB%	BABIP
2018	RAN	ROK	24	0	0	0	3	3	7	3	0	1.3	11.6	9	61.5%	.231
2018	FRI	AA	24	5	6	0	15	15	79^2	76	9	2.6	8.1	72	37.4%	.296
2019	NAS	AAA	25	7	6	1	27	25	135^1	154	24	3.5	7.6	114	35.1%	.316
2020	TEX	MLB	26	2	1	0	8	1	22^1	24	4	2.8	8.5	21	34.3%	.303
2021 FS	TEX	MLB	27	2	3	0	57	0	50	51	9	3.2	7.9	43	35.1%	.295
2021 DC	TEX	MLB	27	2	2	0	53	0	55.3	56	10	3.2	7.9	48	35.1%	.295

Comparables: Ryan Borucki, Matt Hall, Dillon Peters

 Back-end starter. It's a designation that gets tossed around a lot, typically reserved for someone that logs innings, posts an ERA in the high fours, and always seems to find a job. Depending on your era, think Milt Wilcox or Kevin Gross or Miguel Batista. It's awfully early, but Benjamin could be headed to enter those hallowed grounds. He's a lefty (which certainly helps) with a super-spinny fastball that hitters have yet to figure out, slugging just .256 against the 91-94 mph offering this season. There's also room to improve his mediocre strikeout totals, with Benjamin getting more swinging strikes than league average. It didn't hurt when he phased out his changeup in favor of the four-seamer as the season progressed, a classic "trade your worst pitch for your best pitch" swap. Benjamin's career as a big leaguer is obviously in its infancy, but it's also clear that there's a path for him to bounce around, soaking up instantly-forgotten innings for years to come. Pete Smith and Frank Castillo will greet him into the club with open arms.

YEAR	TEAM	LVL	AGE	WHIP	ERA	DRA-	WARP	MPH	FB%	WHF	CSP
2018	RAN	ROK	24	0.57	0.00						
2018	FRI	AA	24	1.24	3.62	91	0.8				
2019	NAS	AAA	25	1.53	5.52	104	2.1				
2020	TEX	MLB	26	1.39	4.84	114	0.0	92.9	50.1%	26.7%	
2021 FS	TEX	MLB	27	1.38	4.71	108	0.0	92.9	50.1%	26.7%	47.9%
2021 DC	TEX	MLB	27	1.38	4.71	108	0.1	92.9	50.1%	26.7%	47.9%

Wes Benjamin, continued

Pitch Shape vs LHH	Pitch Shape vs RHH
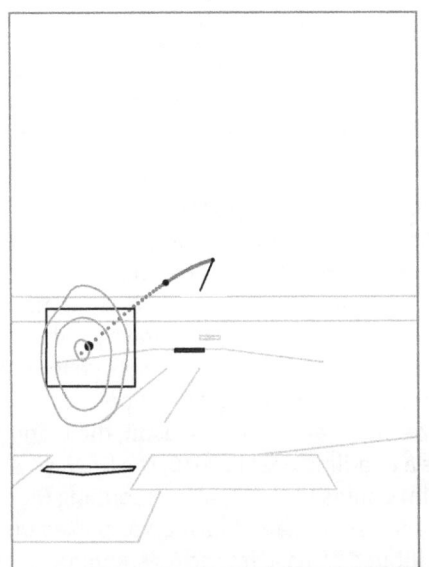	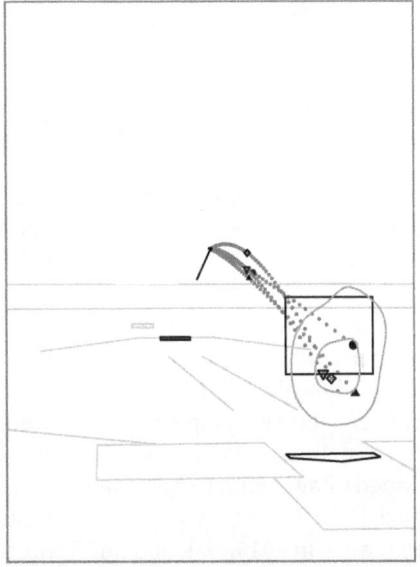

Type	Frequency	Velocity	H Movement	V Movement
● Fastball	50.1%	91 [95]	7.3 [97]	-12.2 [108]
▲ Changeup	12.3%	84.6 [98]	7.1 [124]	-21.2 [117]
▽ Slider	23.1%	85.7 [108]	-2.4 [89]	-28.6 [115]
◇ Curveball	14.4%	78.7 [100]	-5.8 [93]	-51.7 [93]

Jesse Chavez RHP

Born: 08/21/83 Age: 37 Bats: R Throws: R
Height: 6'1" Weight: 175 Origin: Round 42, 2002 Draft (#1252 overall)

YEAR	TEAM	LVL	AGE	W	L	SV	G	GS	IP	H	HR	BB/9	K/9	K	GB%	BABIP
2018	CHC	MLB	34	2	1	4	32	0	39	26	3	1.2	9.7	42	41.7%	.247
2018	TEX	MLB	34	3	1	1	30	0	56¹	58	10	1.9	8.0	50	45.3%	.296
2019	TEX	MLB	35	3	5	1	48	9	78	82	12	2.5	8.3	72	41.6%	.311
2020	TEX	MLB	36	0	0	0	18	0	17	20	6	3.7	6.9	13	39.3%	.280
2021 FS	TEX	MLB	37	2	2	0	57	0	50	50	8	2.8	7.6	42	41.1%	.294

Comparables: Craig Stammen, Matt Belisle, Jim Brewer

There's an old school of thought that the optimist interpretation of being traded is that at least there's one team that actively wants the player. It's meant to be comforting. Chavez has played for nine teams and he's been traded eight times. Running through the returns is both an exercise in "remembering some guys" and a reminder that sometimes the biggest names don't always yield the most productive return. In 2006, the Rangers traded Chavez to Pittsburgh for Kip Wells. Three years later, the Pirates shipped him to the Rays for Akinori Iwamura. Chavez's time in Tampa was short lived, because later that offseason, the team sent him to Atlanta for Rafael Soriano. As a deadline deal in 2010, the Braves traded Chavez with Gregor Blanco and Tim Collins to the Royals, recouping Rick Ankiel and Kyle Farnsworth. Kansas City waived him, and Chavez was picked up by the A's. In 2015, Oakland and Toronto flipped arms, with the A's shipping Chavez north of the border in exchange for Liam Hendriks. The next trade deadline saw Chavez move to Hollywood, joining the Dodgers for Mike Bolsinger. After signing with the Angels the following offseason, and the Rangers a year later, Chavez was traded to the Cubs for Tyler Thomas. He re-signed in Arlington the following offseason. Over the course of those dealings, Chavez amassed 9.5 WARP. After the trades, the guys that he was traded for accumulated 9.1 WARP combined. The lesson: Always trade for Jesse Chavez.

YEAR	TEAM	LVL	AGE	WHIP	ERA	DRA-	WARP	MPH	FB%	WHF	CSP
2018	CHC	MLB	34	0.79	1.15	65	0.9	94.2	92.9%	21.7%	
2018	TEX	MLB	34	1.24	3.51	71	1.1	94.3	69.6%	25.1%	
2019	TEX	MLB	35	1.33	4.85	104	0.4	92.4	70.8%	18.4%	
2020	TEX	MLB	36	1.59	6.88	137	-0.2	92.3	78.7%	15.4%	
2021 FS	TEX	MLB	37	1.32	4.31	100	0.2	92.9	74.7%	19.4%	49.8%

Jesse Chavez, continued

Pitch Shape vs LHH

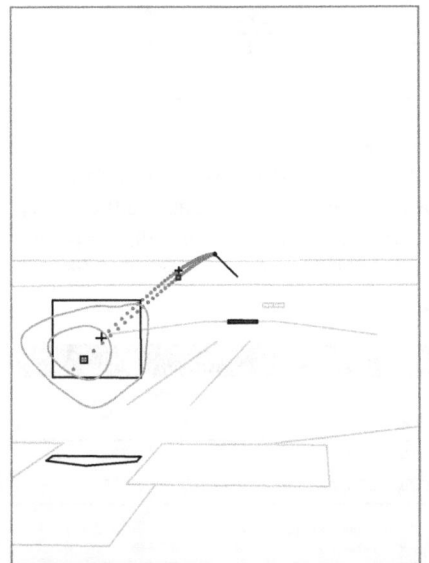

Pitch Shape vs RHH

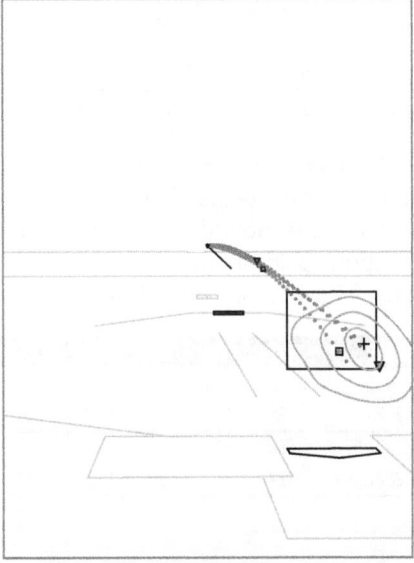

Type	Frequency	Velocity	H Movement	V Movement
● Fastball	3.6%	90.8 [94]	-10 [84]	-15.9 [98]
☐ Sinker	43.9%	91.2 [94]	-14.9 [86]	-21.7 [96]
+ Cutter	31.1%	89.3 [106]	-2 [74]	-18.7 [122]
▲ Changeup	4.9%	85.2 [100]	-15.9 [78]	-30.2 [93]
▽ Slider	16.4%	84 [100]	4.3 [96]	-32.8 [103]

Texas Rangers 2021

Kyle Cody RHP
Born: 08/09/94   Age: 26   Bats: R   Throws: R
Height: 6'7"   Weight: 225   Origin: Round 6, 2016 Draft (#189 overall)

YEAR	TEAM	LVL	AGE	W	L	SV	G	GS	IP	H	HR	BB/9	K/9	K	GB%	BABIP
2018	RAN	ROK	23	0	0	0	2	2	5	2	0	1.8	16.2	9	50.0%	.250
2020	TEX	MLB	25	1	1	0	8	5	22^2	15	1	5.2	7.1	18	47.5%	.233
2021 FS	TEX	MLB	26	9	9	0	26	26	150	144	22	4.4	8.7	144	44.1%	.298
2021 DC	TEX	MLB	26	3	3	0	14	11	48.7	46	7	4.4	8.7	47	44.1%	.298

Comparables: Aaron Blair, Alex Meyer, Jordan Montgomery

The fact that Cody tossed a big-league pitch this season was only slightly more impressive than him throwing a competitive pitch at all, as the tall righty last took the mound in July 2018 thanks to Tommy John surgery. His mid-rotation upside is still there, even if his sparkly 2020 ERA is likely to sink faster than fellow Chippewa Falls native Jack Dawson.

YEAR	TEAM	LVL	AGE	WHIP	ERA	DRA-	WARP	MPH	FB%	WHF	CSP
2018	RAN	ROK	23	0.60	0.00						
2020	TEX	MLB	25	1.24	1.59	98	0.2	96.1	50.3%	21.3%	
2021 FS	TEX	MLB	26	1.45	4.62	104	1.1	96.1	50.3%	21.3%	47.3%
2021 DC	TEX	MLB	26	1.45	4.62	104	0.3	96.1	50.3%	21.3%	47.3%

Kyle Cody, continued

Pitch Shape vs LHH

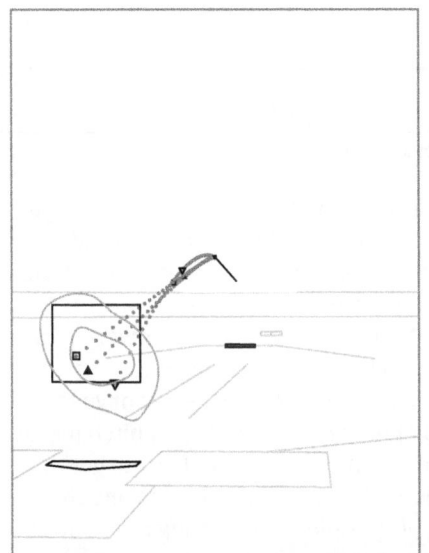

Pitch Shape vs RHH

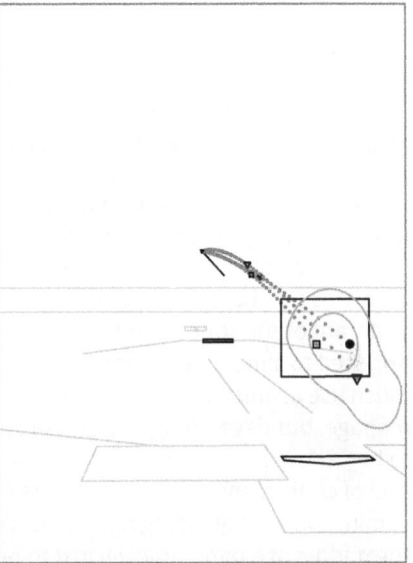

Type	Frequency	Velocity	H Movement	V Movement
● Fastball	30.8%	94.4 [106]	-7.1 [98]	-12.1 [109]
□ Sinker	19.5%	94.6 [111]	-12.9 [102]	-15 [118]
▲ Changeup	12.4%	86.2 [104]	-13.3 [92]	-22.8 [113]
▽ Slider	37.3%	83.3 [97]	3.7 [94]	-40.4 [81]

Dane Dunning   RHP
Born: 12/20/94   Age: 26   Bats: R   Throws: R
Height: 6'4"   Weight: 225   Origin: Round 1, 2016 Draft (#29 overall)

YEAR	TEAM	LVL	AGE	W	L	SV	G	GS	IP	H	HR	BB/9	K/9	K	GB%	BABIP
2018	WS	HI-A	23	1	1	0	4	4	24¹	20	2	1.1	11.5	31	61.3%	.300
2018	BIR	AA	23	5	2	0	11	11	62	57	0	3.3	10.0	69	48.8%	.343
2020	CHW	MLB	25	2	0	0	7	7	34	25	4	3.4	9.3	35	44.6%	.239
2021 FS	TEX	MLB	26	9	8	0	26	26	150	138	21	3.4	9.3	155	43.9%	.298
2021 DC	TEX	MLB	26	7	6	0	22	22	115.7	107	16	3.4	9.3	120	43.9%	.298

Comparables: Tyler Wilson, Sean Manaea, Jordan Montgomery

    A lot of wondrous and remarkable work goes into being as reliably boring as Dunning manages to be. There's a lot of command and a mastery of a wide arsenal that goes into surviving while sitting 91-92 mph with a fastball in 2020. It demands practice and repetition of cutting and riding the heater to every quadrant of the zone to simply earn the status of being "not overpowering" as opposed to simply being dead meat. Most of Dunning's primary weapons aren't much use against left-handers and that's a real shortcoming he will have to manage, but developing a whole second release point and style of pitching, just to be pedestrian against them, is all a remarkable work-around just to get by. And of course, emerging back on the mound, two years after his first elbow sprain, Tommy John surgery, rehab, skipping Triple-A and getting called up in the middle of a pandemic, all just to bore tens of thousands with eating innings the way he was presaged four years ago, is all very remarkable. He'll be boring people in Texas after he was the centerpiece of the Rangers return in a trade for Lance Lynn.

YEAR	TEAM	LVL	AGE	WHIP	ERA	DRA-	WARP	MPH	FB%	WHF	CSP
2018	WS	HI-A	23	0.95	2.59	74	0.5				
2018	BIR	AA	23	1.29	2.76	76	1.3				
2020	CHW	MLB	25	1.12	3.97	91	0.5	93.6	60.6%	27.6%	
2021 FS	TEX	MLB	26	1.31	4.00	93	2.0	93.6	60.6%	27.6%	43.0%
2021 DC	TEX	MLB	26	1.31	4.00	93	1.5	93.6	60.6%	27.6%	43.0%

Dane Dunning, continued

Pitch Shape vs LHH

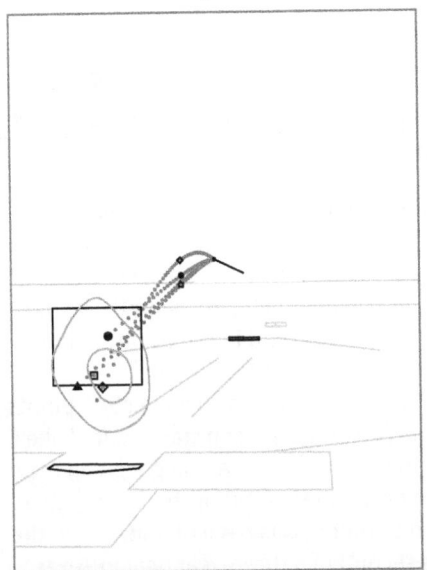

Pitch Shape vs RHH

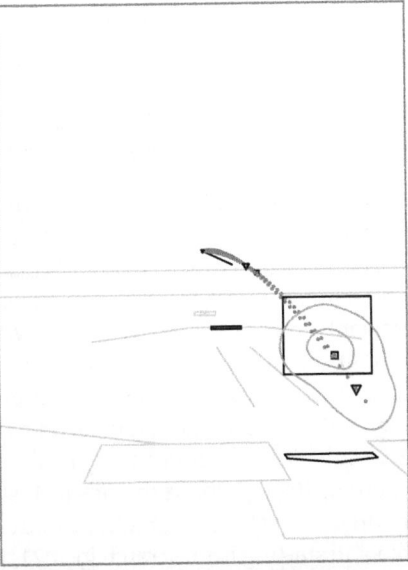

Type	Frequency	Velocity	H Movement	V Movement
● Fastball	20.8%	91.9 [98]	-5.4 [106]	-15.9 [98]
☐ Sinker	39.8%	92.1 [98]	-13.2 [99]	-22.1 [95]
▲ Changeup	10.9%	85.7 [102]	-13.7 [89]	-25.2 [106]
▽ Slider	21.7%	81.7 [90]	2.7 [90]	-40.7 [80]
◇ Curveball	6.8%	78.8 [101]	5.5 [92]	-56.2 [83]

Kyle Gibson RHP

Born: 10/23/87 Age: 33 Bats: R Throws: R
Height: 6'6" Weight: 215 Origin: Round 1, 2009 Draft (#22 overall)

YEAR	TEAM	LVL	AGE	W	L	SV	G	GS	IP	H	HR	BB/9	K/9	K	GB%	BABIP
2018	MIN	MLB	30	10	13	0	32	32	196²	177	23	3.6	8.2	179	49.6%	.286
2019	MIN	MLB	31	13	7	0	34	29	160	175	23	3.1	9.0	160	51.1%	.333
2020	TEX	MLB	32	2	6	0	12	12	67¹	73	12	4.0	7.8	58	51.2%	.313
2021 FS	*TEX*	*MLB*	*33*	*9*	*8*	*0*	*26*	*26*	*150*	*147*	*20*	*3.8*	*8.1*	*135*	*50.4%*	*.299*
2021 DC	*TEX*	*MLB*	*33*	*9*	*8*	*0*	*27*	*27*	*151.3*	*148*	*20*	*3.8*	*8.1*	*136*	*50.4%*	*.299*

Comparables: Jhoulys Chacín, Iván Nova, Chase Anderson

    To say Gibson's first year away from Minnesota was a little bumpy would be akin to saying that Rowan was slightly in over his head with his Worcestershire Pear Tree in the Season 11 bread episode of The Great British Bake Off (read: an understatement). Gibson struggled with his sinker (which, incidentally, so did Rowan), and especially had trouble when getting behind in the count. While that's normally pretty typical for most hurlers, opponents slashed .318/.496/.557 against Gibson in hitters' counts, posting an OPS over 200 points higher than the league average. Sometimes an entire season starts to feel like a 2-0 count. There weren't many positives to take from the campaign; given the chaos of 2020, perhaps the tick he lost on his pitches will show back up with a normal spring? Gibson might be better off dumping this bake of a season in the bin and starting from scratch in 2021, his second of a three-year deal in Texas.

YEAR	TEAM	LVL	AGE	WHIP	ERA	DRA-	WARP	MPH	FB%	WHF	CSP
2018	MIN	MLB	30	1.30	3.62	94	2.5	95.2	57.7%	26.9%	
2019	MIN	MLB	31	1.44	4.84	114	0.3	95.1	50.3%	29.4%	
2020	TEX	MLB	32	1.53	5.35	119	-0.1	93.9	49.4%	23.4%	
2021 FS	*TEX*	*MLB*	*33*	*1.40*	*4.33*	*99*	*1.5*	*94.8*	*52.0%*	*27.1%*	*39.8%*
2021 DC	*TEX*	*MLB*	*33*	*1.40*	*4.33*	*99*	*1.5*	*94.8*	*52.0%*	*27.1%*	*39.8%*

Kyle Gibson, continued

Pitch Shape vs LHH

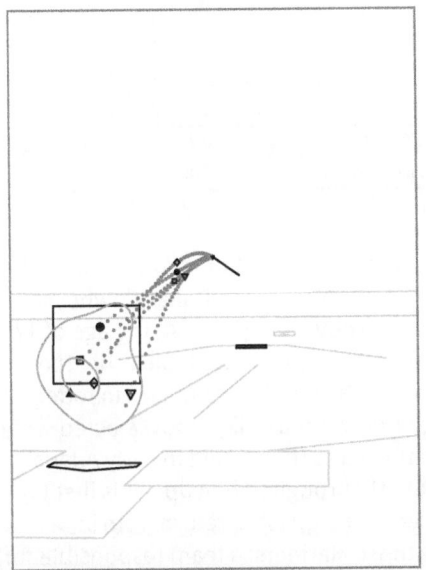

Pitch Shape vs RHH

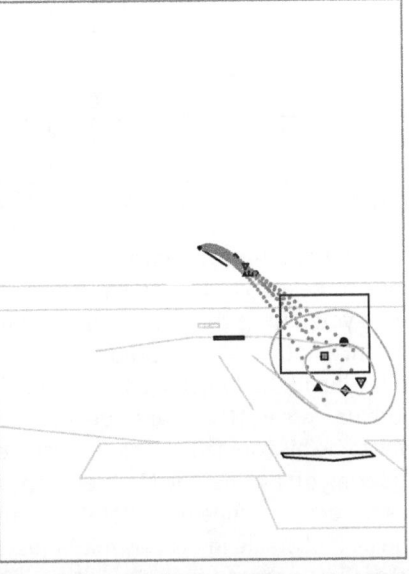

Type	Frequency	Velocity	H Movement	V Movement
● Fastball	14.0%	92.6 [100]	-5.1 [108]	-14.1 [103]
□ Sinker	35.4%	92.3 [100]	-12.4 [105]	-17.7 [109]
▲ Changeup	17.9%	84.5 [98]	-13.1 [92]	-28.3 [98]
▽ Slider	24.7%	83.2 [96]	4.9 [99]	-36.1 [93]
◇ Curveball	7.9%	78.8 [101]	5.6 [92]	-46.9 [103]

Taylor Hearn   LHP

Born: 08/30/94   Age: 26   Bats: L   Throws: L
Height: 6'6"   Weight: 230   Origin: Round 5, 2015 Draft (#164 overall)

YEAR	TEAM	LVL	AGE	W	L	SV	G	GS	IP	H	HR	BB/9	K/9	K	GB%	BABIP
2018	FRI	AA	23	1	2	0	5	5	25	29	5	3.2	11.9	33	36.2%	.375
2018	ALT	AA	23	3	6	0	19	19	104	75	6	3.3	9.3	107	37.7%	.258
2019	NAS	AAA	24	1	3	0	4	4	20	14	3	4.5	11.7	26	26.7%	.262
2019	TEX	MLB	24	0	1	0	1	1	0¹	3	0	108.0	0.0	0	50.0%	.750
2020	TEX	MLB	25	0	0	0	14	0	17¹	13	2	5.7	11.9	23	26.8%	.282
2021 FS	TEX	MLB	26	2	3	0	57	0	50	46	8	4.7	10.4	57	34.4%	.301
2021 DC	TEX	MLB	26	2	3	0	59	0	61.7	56	10	4.7	10.4	71	34.4%	.301

Comparables: Conner Menez, Keegan Akin, Joe Palumbo

Under different circumstances, Hearn's professional debut in Arlington might have come across the street in Cowboy Stadium. Not for the Dallas Cowboys, mind you, but as the latest in a long line of cowboy champions. At the age of 17 Hearn, a native Texan, opted for a new challenge with the hardball rather than following in the footsteps of his grandfather, father, and three uncles in rodeo. In both universes, Hearn was due for a rough ride. After a balky elbow ejected what was to be his rookie 2019 campaign, he returned to the mound in early August, squaring off against the Mariners—the team that roughed him up in his first big-league action. While he certainly triumphed in the quest to return from injury, the next obstacle in his way might just be those Mariners, a team responsible for 10 of the 12 earned runs Hearn has surrendered thus far in his career. Though he's definitely been dealt a rough stock, signs point to Hearn not only being up for the task, but also able to rope success like a, well, you get it.

YEAR	TEAM	LVL	AGE	WHIP	ERA	DRA-	WARP	MPH	FB%	WHF	CSP
2018	FRI	AA	23	1.52	5.04	87	0.3				
2018	ALT	AA	23	1.09	3.12	76	2.1				
2019	NAS	AAA	24	1.20	4.05	59	0.7				
2019	TEX	MLB	24	21.00	108.00	38	0.0	92.8	69.2%	8.3%	
2020	TEX	MLB	25	1.38	3.63	102	0.1	97.2	60.5%	24.5%	
2021 FS	TEX	MLB	26	1.44	4.69	105	0.1	96.9	61.1%	23.4%	49.1%
2021 DC	TEX	MLB	26	1.44	4.69	105	0.2	96.9	61.1%	23.4%	49.1%

Taylor Hearn, continued

Pitch Shape vs LHH

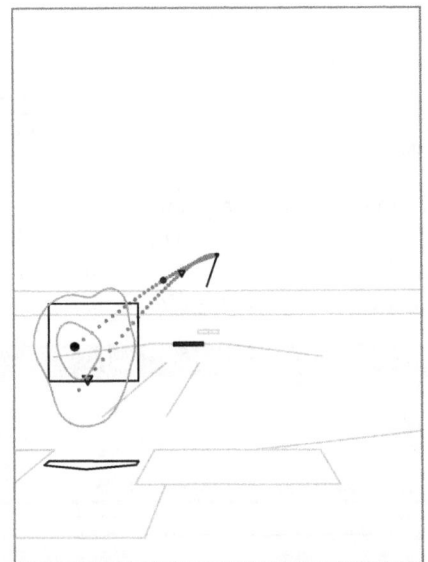

Pitch Shape vs RHH

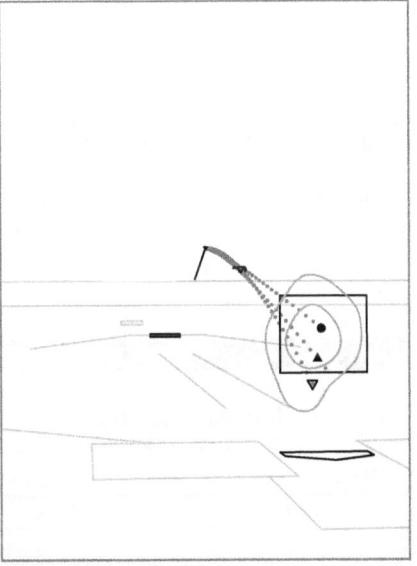

Type	Frequency	Velocity	H Movement	V Movement
● Fastball	60.5%	95.1 [108]	5 [108]	-11.5 [110]
▲ Changeup	11.4%	85.1 [100]	8.7 [116]	-25 [107]
▽ Slider	28.1%	83.9 [100]	-5.2 [100]	-30.8 [109]

Jimmy Herget   RHP

Born: 09/09/93   Age: 27   Bats: R   Throws: R
Height: 6'3"   Weight: 170   Origin: Round 6, 2015 Draft (#175 overall)

YEAR	TEAM	LVL	AGE	W	L	SV	G	GS	IP	H	HR	BB/9	K/9	K	GB%	BABIP
2018	LOU	AAA	24	1	3	0	50	0	59^2	59	5	3.2	9.8	65	35.3%	.329
2019	LOU	AAA	25	3	4	2	48	0	58^2	41	7	5.5	10.4	68	34.5%	.246
2019	CIN	MLB	25	0	0	0	5	0	6^1	8	2	4.3	0.0	0	21.7%	.286
2020	TEX	MLB	26	1	0	0	20	1	19^2	13	2	6.4	7.8	17	35.2%	.216
2021 FS	TEX	MLB	27	2	3	0	57	0	50	47	8	4.3	8.9	49	34.5%	.290

Comparables: Jacob Rhame, Nick Rumbelow, Trevor Gott

After being scooped up off of waivers from Cincinnati, Herget made 20 appearances for the Rangers, threading the needle, walking the tightrope, and tiptoeing through a minefield of excess walks. Pretty impressive to do them all at the same time; more so to do it and escape with such a tidy ERA.

YEAR	TEAM	LVL	AGE	WHIP	ERA	DRA-	WARP	MPH	FB%	WHF	CSP
2018	LOU	AAA	24	1.34	3.47	80	0.8				
2019	LOU	AAA	25	1.31	2.91	64	1.8				
2019	CIN	MLB	25	1.74	4.26	174	-0.2	94.7	50.7%	18.8%	
2020	TEX	MLB	26	1.37	3.20	117	0.0	95.2	54.3%	25.7%	
2021 FS	TEX	MLB	27	1.42	4.77	107	0.1	95.1	53.9%	24.8%	48.8%

Jimmy Herget, continued

Pitch Shape vs LHH

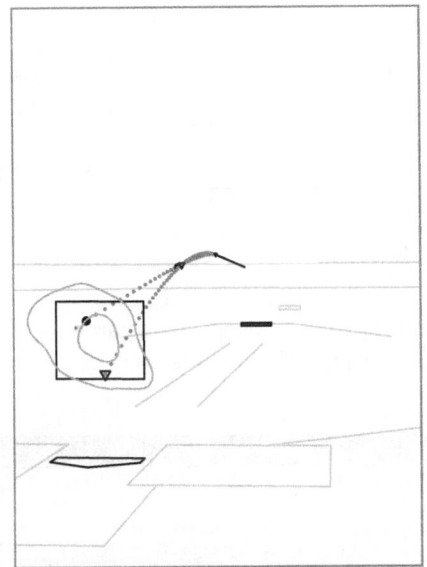

Pitch Shape vs RHH

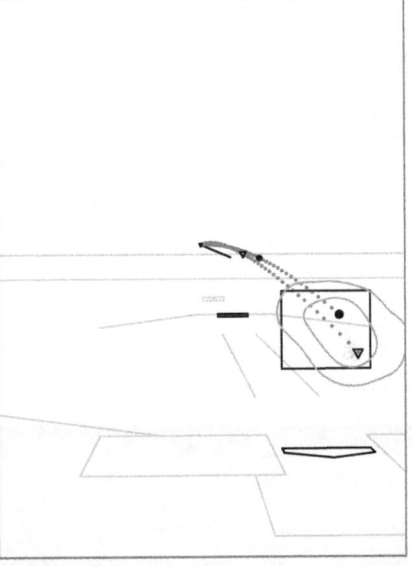

Type	Frequency	Velocity	H Movement	V Movement
● Fastball	43.5%	93.6 [103]	-13.3 [69]	-18.8 [90]
□ Sinker	10.2%	90.9 [92]	-14.8 [87]	-26.1 [82]
▲ Changeup	3.4%	85.4 [101]	-13.3 [92]	-29.2 [95]
▽ Slider	40.7%	81.8 [90]	5.8 [102]	-35.4 [95]

Jonathan Hernández   RHP

Born: 07/06/96   Age: 25   Bats: R   Throws: R
Height: 6'3"   Weight: 190   Origin: International Free Agent, 2013

YEAR	TEAM	LVL	AGE	W	L	SV	G	GS	IP	H	HR	BB/9	K/9	K	GB%	BABIP
2018	DE	HI-A	21	4	2	0	10	10	57^1	37	6	2.7	12.1	77	50.8%	.263
2018	FRI	AA	21	4	4	0	12	12	64	58	6	5.1	8.0	57	50.6%	.299
2019	FRI	AA	22	5	9	0	22	16	96	100	11	3.6	8.9	95	47.1%	.331
2019	TEX	MLB	22	2	1	0	9	2	16^2	14	3	7.0	10.3	19	52.2%	.256
2020	TEX	MLB	23	5	1	0	27	0	31	24	2	2.3	9.0	31	45.1%	.278
2021 FS	TEX	MLB	24	2	2	11	57	0	50	46	6	4.9	9.1	50	45.5%	.300
2021 DC	TEX	MLB	24	2	3	11	59	0	61.7	57	8	4.9	9.1	62	45.5%	.300

Comparables: Touki Toussaint, Zack Littell, Tyrell Jenkins

Devin Williams, James Karinchak, Tejay Antone, and...Hernández? Through the first month of the season, it certainly looked as though the latter was planting his flag as one of the most dominant young relievers in the game. As for the second month of the season, well, let's just say he's not quite there yet. There are plenty of months still to come.

YEAR	TEAM	LVL	AGE	WHIP	ERA	DRA-	WARP	MPH	FB%	WHF	CSP
2018	DE	HI-A	21	0.94	2.20	50	2.0				
2018	FRI	AA	21	1.47	4.92	90	0.6				
2019	FRI	AA	22	1.44	5.16	117	-1.0				
2019	TEX	MLB	22	1.62	4.32	103	0.1	98.7	48.5%	32.6%	
2020	TEX	MLB	23	1.03	2.90	84	0.5	99.4	47.5%	33.8%	
2021 FS	TEX	MLB	24	1.48	4.57	102	0.2	99.2	47.8%	33.4%	41.5%
2021 DC	TEX	MLB	24	1.48	4.57	102	0.3	99.2	47.8%	33.4%	41.5%

Jonathan Hernández, continued

Pitch Shape vs LHH

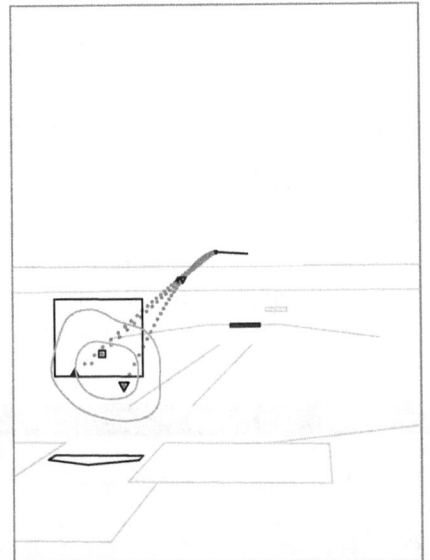

Pitch Shape vs RHH

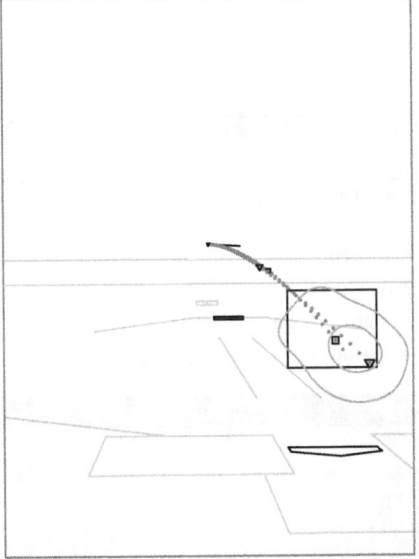

Type	Frequency	Velocity	H Movement	V Movement
□ Sinker	47.1%	97.9 [128]	-16 [79]	-18 [108]
▲ Changeup	12.6%	91 [123]	-13.3 [91]	-18.3 [125]
▽ Slider	39.7%	89.3 [124]	3.8 [94]	-27 [120]

Texas Rangers 2021

John King LHP
Born: 09/14/94   Age: 26   Bats: L   Throws: L
Height: 6'2"   Weight: 215   Origin: Round 10, 2017 Draft (#314 overall)

YEAR	TEAM	LVL	AGE	W	L	SV	G	GS	IP	H	HR	BB/9	K/9	K	GB%	BABIP
2018	RAN	ROK	23	0	0	0	1	1	1^2	3	0	5.4	5.4	1	71.4%	.429
2018	SPO	SS	23	0	0	0	1	1	3	5	0	0.0	6.0	2	25.0%	.417
2019	HIC	LO-A	24	1	2	0	5	5	26^1	31	1	0.7	9.9	29	63.3%	.385
2019	DE	HI-A	24	2	4	0	14	14	71	59	4	1.4	7.7	61	54.8%	.282
2020	TEX	MLB	25	1	0	0	6	0	10^1	13	2	3.5	7.8	9	55.6%	.324
2021 FS	TEX	MLB	26	2	2	0	57	0	50	51	7	3.3	7.4	41	47.0%	.301
2021 DC	TEX	MLB	26	0	1	0	6	3	12.7	13	1	3.3	7.4	10	47.0%	.301

Comparables: Randy Rosario, Anthony Kay, Gregory Soto

Another result of the suddenly popular A-ball-to-majors pipeline, the hard-throwing lefty King earned all nine of his strikeouts swinging. Should this trend continue throughout his career, a 100 percent swinging-strikeout rate would likely be a major-league record.

YEAR	TEAM	LVL	AGE	WHIP	ERA	DRA-	WARP	MPH	FB%	WHF	CSP
2018	RAN	ROK	23	2.40	5.40						
2018	SPO	SS	23	1.67	6.00	300	-0.4				
2019	HIC	LO-A	24	1.25	3.42	117	-0.2				
2019	DE	HI-A	24	0.99	2.03	79	1.0				
2020	TEX	MLB	25	1.65	6.10	91	0.1	94.7	63.4%	19.5%	
2021 FS	TEX	MLB	26	1.39	4.46	103	0.1	94.7	63.4%	19.5%	49.5%
2021 DC	TEX	MLB	26	1.39	4.46	103	0.1	94.7	63.4%	19.5%	49.5%

John King, continued

Pitch Shape vs LHH

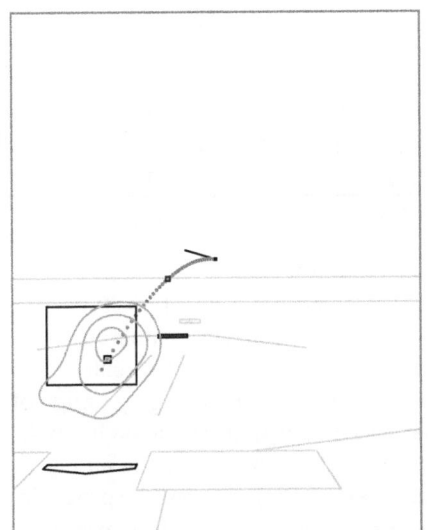

Pitch Shape vs RHH

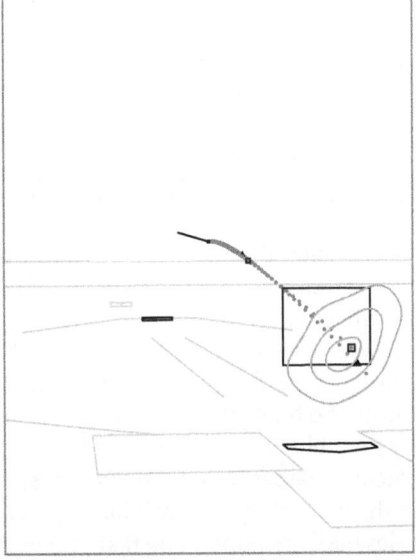

Type	Frequency	Velocity	H Movement	V Movement
☐ Sinker	63.4%	93.2 [104]	14.5 [90]	-26.3 [81]
▲ Changeup	17.2%	78.6 [74]	12.3 [97]	-33.4 [84]
▽ Slider	18.8%	82.1 [92]	-2.8 [91]	-41 [79]

Jordan Lyles RHP

Born: 10/19/90   Age: 30   Bats: R   Throws: R
Height: 6'5"   Weight: 230   Origin: Round 1, 2008 Draft (#38 overall)

YEAR	TEAM	LVL	AGE	W	L	SV	G	GS	IP	H	HR	BB/9	K/9	K	GB%	BABIP
2018	MIL	MLB	27	1	0	0	11	0	16.1	12	0	5.0	12.1	22	42.1%	.316
2018	SD	MLB	27	2	4	0	24	8	71.1	71	12	2.4	7.8	62	45.7%	.291
2019	MIL	MLB	28	7	1	0	11	11	58.2	43	9	3.4	8.6	56	38.8%	.227
2019	PIT	MLB	28	5	7	0	17	17	82.1	88	16	3.6	9.8	90	41.4%	.327
2020	TEX	MLB	29	1	6	0	12	9	57.2	67	12	3.6	5.6	36	40.5%	.286
2021 FS	TEX	MLB	30	9	9	0	26	26	150	153	24	3.5	7.4	123	41.9%	.294
2021 DC	TEX	MLB	30	8	8	0	25	25	129.3	132	21	3.5	7.4	106	41.9%	.294

Comparables: Chris Stratton, Vin Mazzaro, Kendall Graveman

They should really make the whole plane out of the black box, and Lyles should make his whole career out of being a Brewer. In two separate stints, Lyles went 8-1 with Milwaukee, with a 2.64 ERA and 78 strikeouts in 75 innings. Everywhere else, well, made the heart grow fonder. Perhaps he just really loved a fresh, icy cold Miller Lite after each game, or maybe he couldn't get enough of the jumbo burgers at Kopp's Frozen Custard. As a dual-sport star in high school, it's possible that Lyles dreamed of jumping in a Lyft to Lambeau Field and catching passes from Aaron Rodgers, or as an avid golfer, he liked the proximity to the majestic greens of Whistling Straits or Erin Hills. Whatever the reason, Lyles had a disappointing first year with the Rangers, having difficulty finding consistent velocity and shying away from the primarily two-pitch arsenal that found so much success in 2019. The good news is that his curveball was still pretty good, inducing a decent number of whiffs and holding opposing offenses to putrid slugging numbers. The bad news is that his fastball got tattooed, leading to questions as to whether its previous success was dreamed in a PBR and bratwurst-induced stupor.

YEAR	TEAM	LVL	AGE	WHIP	ERA	DRA-	WARP	MPH	FB%	WHF	CSP
2018	MIL	MLB	27	1.29	3.31	57	0.5	96.2	47.6%	31.2%	
2018	SD	MLB	27	1.26	4.29	131	-0.6	95.7	48.8%	21.5%	
2019	MIL	MLB	28	1.11	2.45	78	1.2	94.1	50.6%	21.5%	
2019	PIT	MLB	28	1.47	5.36	92	1.1	94.4	52.9%	24.6%	
2020	TEX	MLB	29	1.56	7.02	155	-1.2	94.1	48.1%	16.9%	
2021 FS	TEX	MLB	30	1.41	4.65	106	0.9	94.5	50.2%	21.3%	46.9%
2021 DC	TEX	MLB	30	1.41	4.65	106	0.7	94.5	50.2%	21.3%	46.9%

Jordan Lyles, continued

Pitch Shape vs LHH

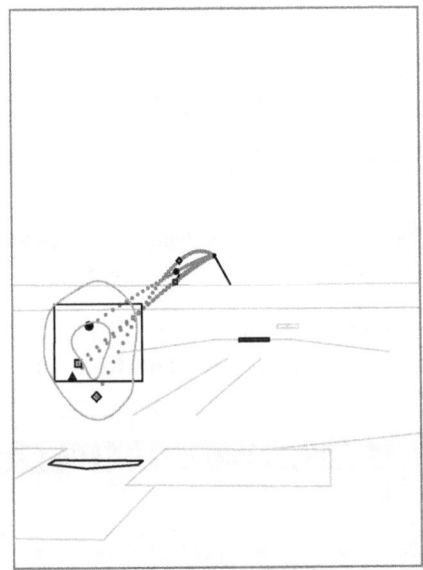

Pitch Shape vs RHH

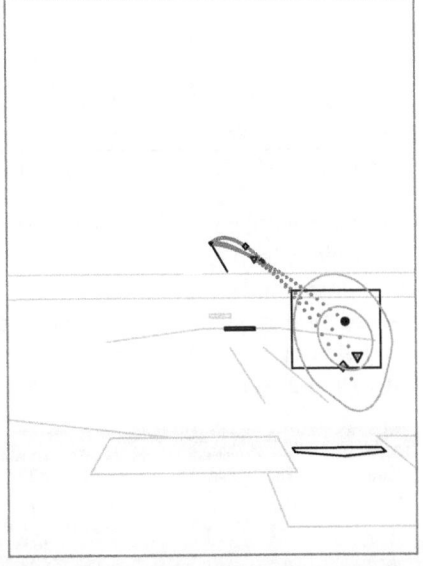

Type	Frequency	Velocity	H Movement	V Movement
● Fastball	43.7%	92.4 [100]	-7 [99]	-13.2 [106]
□ Sinker	4.3%	91.6 [96]	-12.9 [101]	-17.5 [110]
▲ Changeup	9.4%	86.9 [107]	-11.9 [99]	-23.7 [110]
▽ Slider	12.7%	85.8 [108]	4 [95]	-29.9 [111]
◇ Curveball	29.8%	79.9 [105]	5.4 [91]	-52.1 [92]

Brett Martin LHP

Born: 04/28/95   Age: 26   Bats: L   Throws: L
Height: 6'4"   Weight: 200   Origin: Round 4, 2014 Draft (#126 overall)

YEAR	TEAM	LVL	AGE	W	L	SV	G	GS	IP	H	HR	BB/9	K/9	K	GB%	BABIP
2018	FRI	AA	23	2	10	0	29	15	89	138	7	2.9	9.7	96	48.2%	.449
2019	NAS	AAA	24	0	0	1	10	0	12²	10	0	2.8	13.5	19	57.1%	.357
2019	TEX	MLB	24	2	3	0	51	2	62¹	72	7	2.6	9.0	62	53.0%	.340
2020	TEX	MLB	25	1	1	0	15	0	14²	8	2	5.5	4.9	8	50.0%	.143
2021 FS	TEX	MLB	26	2	2	0	57	0	50	49	6	3.4	8.2	45	49.5%	.299
2021 DC	TEX	MLB	26	2	3	0	59	0	61.7	60	8	3.4	8.2	55	49.5%	.299

Comparables: Randy Rosario, Jesus Tinoco, Conner Menez

You know the part of the horror movie where the killer is sneaking up behind an oblivious teenage victim, ready to attack, when said victim somehow slips away unscathed? That's kind of like Martin's 2020 campaign, where the lefty walked more guys than he struck out, stranded runners at an unsustainable clip, and held opponents beneath the Mendoza Line on balls in play only to escape with a sub-2.00 ERA.

YEAR	TEAM	LVL	AGE	WHIP	ERA	DRA-	WARP	MPH	FB%	WHF	CSP
2018	FRI	AA	23	1.88	7.28	95	0.5				
2019	NAS	AAA	24	1.11	0.71	37	0.5				
2019	TEX	MLB	24	1.44	4.76	91	0.6	95.6	52.2%	27.8%	
2020	TEX	MLB	25	1.16	1.84	122	0.0	95.7	53.2%	17.3%	
2021 FS	TEX	MLB	26	1.36	4.11	96	0.3	95.6	52.4%	25.2%	47.9%
2021 DC	TEX	MLB	26	1.36	4.11	96	0.4	95.6	52.4%	25.2%	47.9%

Brett Martin, continued

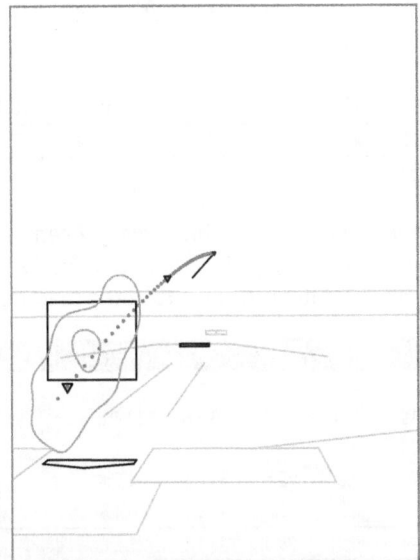

Pitch Shape vs LHH

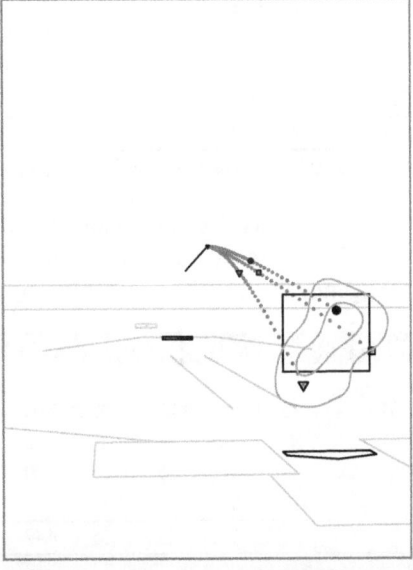

Pitch Shape vs RHH

Type	Frequency	Velocity	H Movement	V Movement
● Fastball	32.9%	94.1 [105]	5.3 [107]	-13.3 [105]
□ Sinker	20.3%	94.3 [110]	13.4 [97]	-17.7 [109]
▽ Slider	33.8%	87.6 [116]	-1.5 [86]	-28.5 [115]
◇ Curveball	13.1%	83.3 [118]	-0.8 [73]	-39.7 [119]

Texas Rangers 2021

Luis Perdomo RHP
Born: 05/09/93 Age: 28 Bats: R Throws: R
Height: 6'2" Weight: 201 Origin: International Free Agent, 2003

YEAR	TEAM	LVL	AGE	W	L	SV	G	GS	IP	H	HR	BB/9	K/9	K	GB%	BABIP
2018	ELP	AAA	25	6	3	0	13	13	75	72	12	2.5	7.3	61	56.5%	.284
2018	SD	MLB	25	1	6	0	12	10	44^2	62	4	4.4	7.9	39	43.1%	.392
2019	ELP	AAA	26	2	1	1	11	0	15	21	3	2.4	10.2	17	51.1%	.419
2019	SD	MLB	26	2	4	0	47	1	72	69	6	2.2	6.9	55	52.0%	.296
2020	SD	MLB	27	0	0	0	10	1	17^1	13	3	5.2	8.3	16	60.4%	.222
2021 FS	TEX	MLB	28	2	2	0	57	0	50	49	6	3.2	8.2	45	53.2%	.297

Comparables: Daniel Mengden, Jakob Junis, Jorge López

Perdomo will miss the season after undergoing Tommy John surgery. Even before he was released in November, he was unnervingly close to qualifying for free agency despite not accomplishing a whole lot in his five years in the majors.

YEAR	TEAM	LVL	AGE	WHIP	ERA	DRA-	WARP	MPH	FB%	WHF	CSP
2018	ELP	AAA	25	1.24	3.72	88	1.2				
2018	SD	MLB	25	1.88	7.05	145	-0.6	95.0	63.1%	19.4%	
2019	ELP	AAA	26	1.67	3.60	103	0.2				
2019	SD	MLB	26	1.21	4.00	88	0.8	95.6	54.5%	19.9%	
2020	SD	MLB	27	1.33	5.71	91	0.2	95.5	42.8%	26.4%	
2021 FS	TEX	MLB	28	1.35	4.17	98	0.3	95.5	53.8%	21.2%	48.2%

Luis Perdomo, continued

Pitch Shape vs LHH

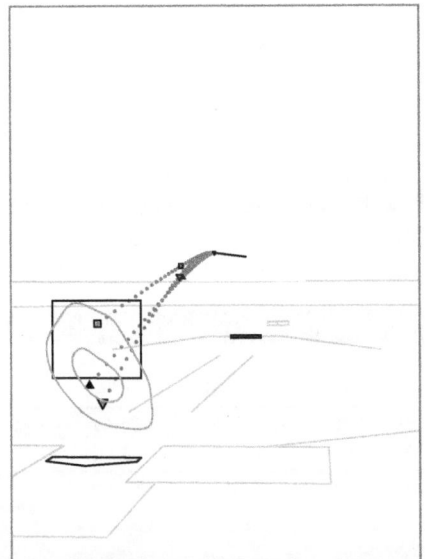

Pitch Shape vs RHH

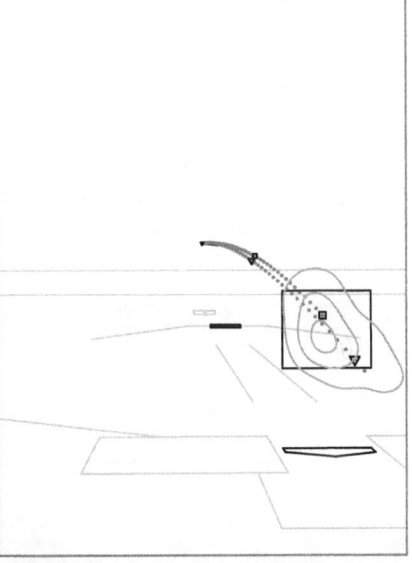

Type	Frequency	Velocity	H Movement	V Movement
☐ Sinker	42.4%	94 [108]	-13.7 [95]	-19.9 [102]
▲ Changeup	22.5%	88.4 [113]	-13 [93]	-27.2 [101]
▽ Slider	34.8%	86.4 [111]	1 [84]	-33.7 [100]

Joely Rodríguez LHP
Born: 11/14/91 Age: 29 Bats: L Throws: L
Height: 6'1" Weight: 200 Origin: International Free Agent, 2009

YEAR	TEAM	LVL	AGE	W	L	SV	G	GS	IP	H	HR	BB/9	K/9	K	GB%	BABIP
2018	NOR	AAA	26	5	3	2	33	1	49[1]	49	1	3.3	9.5	52	56.2%	.333
2020	TEX	MLB	28	0	0	0	12	0	12[2]	8	0	3.6	12.1	17	50.0%	.276
2021 FS	TEX	MLB	29	2	2	0	57	0	50	44	5	4.3	10.1	56	51.5%	.306
2021 DC	TEX	MLB	29	2	2	0	59	0	61.7	55	6	4.3	10.1	69	51.5%	.306

Comparables: Kyle Ryan, Luke Jackson, Mike Mayers

It took a two-year excursion to Japan (and a shiny new changeup) to revitalize Rodríguez, who transformed from afterthought to legit lefty arm out of the pen in 2020. It was one of the biggest reclamation projects in Tokyo since the unveiling of Tokyo Waterfront City way back in, uh, also 2020. It was a long year.

YEAR	TEAM	LVL	AGE	WHIP	ERA	DRA-	WARP	MPH	FB%	WHF	CSP
2018	NOR	AAA	26	1.36	4.56	69	1.0				
2020	TEX	MLB	28	1.03	2.13	74	0.3	96.4	67.2%	26.3%	
2021 FS	TEX	MLB	29	1.37	3.88	91	0.5	96.4	67.2%	26.3%	47.1%
2021 DC	TEX	MLB	29	1.37	3.88	91	0.6	96.4	67.2%	26.3%	47.1%

Joely Rodríguez, continued

Pitch Shape vs LHH

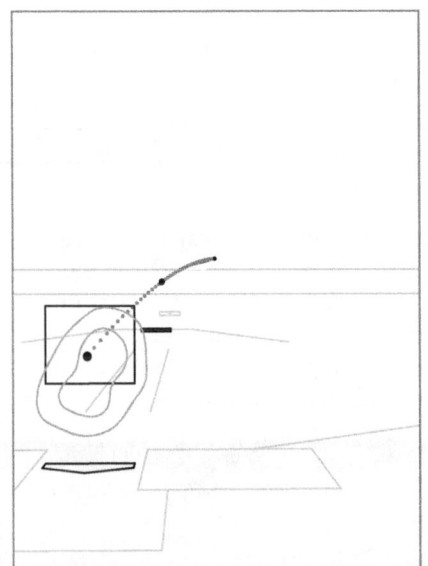

Pitch Shape vs RHH

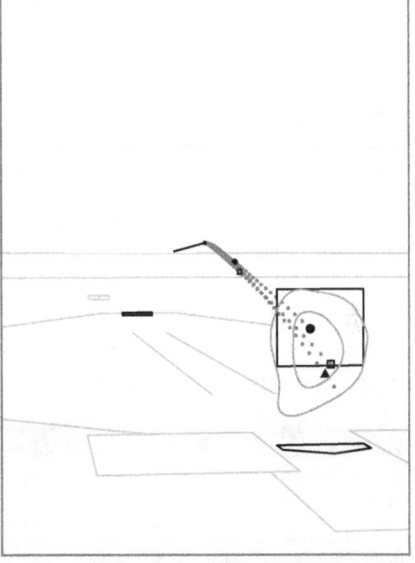

Type	Frequency	Velocity	H Movement	V Movement
● Fastball	35.8%	94.6 [106]	12.5 [72]	-18.3 [91]
☐ Sinker	31.5%	95 [113]	16.3 [76]	-22.3 [94]
▲ Changeup	30.2%	89.4 [117]	10.3 [107]	-30.9 [91]

Texas Rangers 2021

Nick Vincent RHP
Born: 07/12/86   Age: 34   Bats: R   Throws: R
Height: 5'10"   Weight: 185   Origin: Round 18, 2008 Draft (#555 overall)

YEAR	TEAM	LVL	AGE	W	L	SV	G	GS	IP	H	HR	BB/9	K/9	K	GB%	BABIP
2018	SEA	MLB	31	4	4	0	62	1	56^1	50	7	2.4	8.9	56	29.7%	.274
2019	LHV	AAA	32	0	0	0	10	0	12^1	9	1	0.7	9.5	13	35.3%	.242
2019	SF	MLB	32	0	2	0	18	1	30^2	36	7	2.3	8.8	30	39.2%	.322
2019	PHI	MLB	32	1	2	0	14	0	14	11	1	2.6	10.9	17	35.3%	.303
2020	MIA	MLB	33	1	2	3	21	0	22^1	23	5	2.4	6.9	17	33.8%	.286
2021 FS	TEX	MLB	34	2	2	0	57	0	50	46	7	2.1	8.1	44	34.7%	.276

Comparables: Fernando Salas, Huston Street, Keith Foulke

In an age of high-velocity fastball/slider arms, Vincent has carved out a long career with one weird trick: using lots of fastballs and cutters mostly in the high-80s, less frequently in the low-90s. He's somehow been effective more often than not, even through the peripatetic NRI phase of his career. The margins are thin for Vincent as an increasingly dinger-prone pitcher heading into his mid-30s, but he's been beating the odds since 2012.

YEAR	TEAM	LVL	AGE	WHIP	ERA	DRA-	WARP	MPH	FB%	WHF	CSP
2018	SEA	MLB	31	1.15	3.99	79	0.9	90.7	96.0%	24.4%	
2019	LHV	AAA	32	0.81	1.46	47	0.5				
2019	SF	MLB	32	1.43	5.58	115	-0.1	90.4	94.8%	25.5%	
2019	PHI	MLB	32	1.07	1.93	83	0.2	90.0	96.6%	21.3%	
2020	MIA	MLB	33	1.30	4.43	129	-0.2	90.3	87.9%	21.1%	
2021 FS	TEX	MLB	34	1.16	3.55	87	0.6	90.4	93.3%	23.4%	50.7%

Nick Vincent, continued

Pitch Shape vs LHH

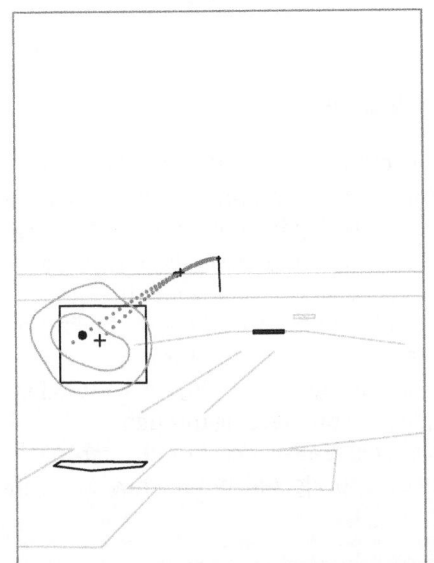

Pitch Shape vs RHH

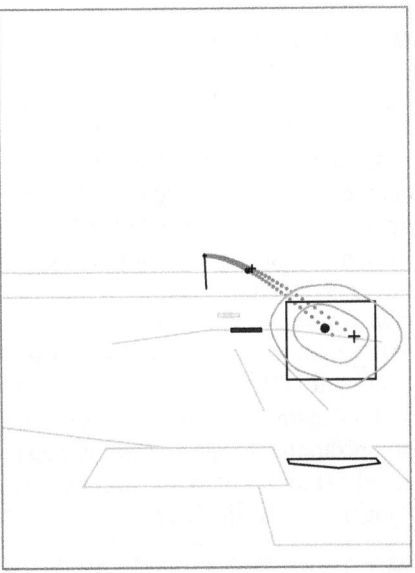

Type	Frequency	Velocity	H Movement	V Movement
● Fastball	40.9%	89.4 [90]	-5 [108]	-15.4 [99]
☐ Sinker	5.6%	89.6 [86]	-12.1 [107]	-18.6 [106]
+ Cutter	41.5%	87.7 [96]	1 [94]	-19.8 [117]
▲ Changeup	8.0%	83.3 [93]	-11.9 [99]	-27 [101]
▽ Slider	4.0%	82.9 [95]	4.7 [98]	-32.9 [102]

PLAYER COMMENTS WITHOUT GRAPHS

Maximo Acosta SS
Born: 10/29/02   Age: 18   Bats: R   Throws: R
Height: 6'1"   Weight: 170   Origin: International Free Agent, 2019

    Among the many reasons to be bummed out by the cancellation of minor-league baseball for 2020 is the lost development time for promising players. Acosta was set for his first year stateside after signing the second-largest bonus the Rangers shelled out during the 2019 J2 period, his $1.65 million trailing only Bayron Lora among the international free agent class. Heading into this season, it was arguably Acosta who had more buzz, blending a decent conceptualization of the zone with power and speed, and drawing early Gleyber Torres comps. There's definitely a nonzero chance that, had he played in 2020, we'd be talking about Acosta as one of the "Next Dudes", rapidly progressing through organizational levels and soaring up prospect lists alike. Acosta will enter 2021 at a different point in his career than previously projected, but the raw talent the Rangers saw is still there.

Luisangel Acuna SS
Born: 03/12/02 Age: 19 Bats: R Throws: R
Height: 5'10" Weight: 155 Origin: International Free Agent, 2018

YEAR	TEAM	LVL	AGE	PA	R	2B	3B	HR	RBI	BB	K	SB	CS	AVG/OBP/SLG
2019	DSL RGR1	ROK	17	240	61	11	3	2	29	34	26	17	6	.342/.438/.455
2021								No projection						

Throughout history, brothers have cut their individual paths to fame in the same field: John Wilkes and Edwin Booth, Richard and David Attenborough, Noah and Liam Gallagher. It's not exactly commonplace, but also not exceedingly rare, although the quality of the combinations do vary greatly. Baseball provides its fair share of familial duos running the gamut of effectiveness and acclaim. At one, more evenly successful end, you have Sandy and Roberto Alomar, or the more modern Corey and Kyle Seager. But for every evenly matched set, there's also a Cal and Billy Ripken or Jose and Ozzie Canseco-type mismatch of production. When the Rangers signed Acuna out of Venezuela in July 2018 for a little over $400,000 (more than quadrupling the bonus of his brother, Ronald Jr., from 2014), they added a new sibling rivalry to the ranks. Only time will tell whether the Acuñas will be the Uptons or Giambis, but if Luisangel's hot start, including a near-.900 OPS as a 17-year-old in the Dominican Summer League, is any indication, the Acuñas could be a balanced familial force the likes of which baseball hasn't yet seen.

YEAR	TEAM	LVL	AGE	PA	DRC+	BABIP	BRR	FRAA	WARP
2019	DSL RGR1	ROK	17	240		.381			
2021					No projection				

Sherten Apostel 3B

Born: 03/11/99 Age: 22 Bats: R Throws: R
Height: 6'4" Weight: 235 Origin: International Free Agent, 2018

YEAR	TEAM	LVL	AGE	PA	R	2B	3B	HR	RBI	BB	K	SB	CS	AVG/OBP/SLG
2018	BRS	ROK	19	175	28	7	0	7	26	32	42	3	1	.259/.406/.460
2018	SPO	SS	19	49	7	1	0	1	10	9	8	0	1	.351/.469/.459
2019	HIC	LO-A	20	319	38	13	1	15	43	28	71	2	1	.258/.332/.470
2019	DE	HI-A	20	159	18	5	1	4	16	23	49	0	0	.237/.352/.378
2020	TEX	MLB	21	21	1	1	0	0	0	1	9	0	0	.100/.143/.150
2021 FS	TEX	MLB	22	600	61	22	2	16	59	56	222	2	1	.195/.277/.334
2021 DC	TEX	MLB	22	189	19	7	0	5	18	17	70	0	1	.195/.277/.334

Comparables: Josh Bell, Will Middlebrooks, Jeimer Candelario

While call-up stories aren't one-size-fits-all, they typically sound something like this: Prospect gets call, prospect calls loved ones, prospect meets team in appointed location, prospect prepares with team before his debut. Easy, right? Thanks to 2020, Apostel's call up was a bit different. After a typical practice day at the team's alternate site, the 21-year-old went home, made some lunch, and scrolled through Netflix before finally drifting off for a nap. He awoke to the buzzing of his phone and several missed calls from the Rangers' director of minor league operations, whereupon Apostel learned he needed to be at the stadium, ready to play, in 20 minutes for the second half of a doubleheader. Despite hitting every red light on the way, Apostel debuted at the hot corner, making his first appearance as a big leaguer after not spending any time at a level more advanced than High-A. He even got a hit in the seventh inning. It's probably unlikely that Apostel will start the 2021 season in Arlington, but his patient approach at the dish combined with some budding pop should put him in position to be a fixture for the Rangers at third base in the not-too-distant future, depending on traffic.

YEAR	TEAM	LVL	AGE	PA	DRC+	BABIP	BRR	FRAA	WARP
2018	BRS	ROK	19	175		.319			
2018	SPO	SS	19	49	201	.400	0.0	3B(8): -0.6	0.4
2019	HIC	LO-A	20	319	119	.290	-3.0	3B(70): 1.6, 1B(12): 0.0	1.4
2019	DE	HI-A	20	159	116	.341	1.6	3B(41): 1.4	1.1
2020	TEX	MLB	21	21	63	.182	-0.1	1B(5): 0.3, 3B(2): -0.2	-0.1
2021 FS	TEX	MLB	22	600	66	.298	-0.5	3B 0, 1B 1	-1.5
2021 DC	TEX	MLB	22	189	66	.298	-0.2	3B 0, 1B 0	-0.5

Drew Butera C

Born: 08/09/83 Age: 37 Bats: R Throws: R
Height: 6'1" Weight: 212 Origin: Round 5, 2005 Draft (#149 overall)

YEAR	TEAM	LVL	AGE	PA	R	2B	3B	HR	RBI	BB	K	SB	CS	AVG/OBP/SLG
2018	KC	MLB	34	166	11	9	0	2	18	13	37	0	0	.188/.259/.289
2018	COL	MLB	34	16	2	0	0	1	3	2	2	0	0	.214/.312/.429
2019	ABQ	AAA	35	262	38	16	2	9	40	33	55	2	0	.300/.389/.511
2019	COL	MLB	35	49	6	3	0	0	3	4	14	0	0	.163/.229/.233
2020	COL	MLB	36	43	4	2	0	0	4	2	11	0	0	.154/.190/.205
2021 FS	TEX	MLB	37	600	53	20	2	14	58	45	169	1	1	.200/.268/.324

Comparables: Mike DiFelice, Ron Tingley, Jamie Quirk

You know when you have a tube of toothpaste and you squeeze it really hard to get those last dabs out, delaying the need to acquire a completely new tube of toothpaste? Anyway, Butera was in the majors last year.

YEAR	TEAM	P. COUNT	FRM RUNS	BLK RUNS	THRW RUNS	TOT RUNS
2018	COL	751	-0.7	-0.1	0.0	-0.9
2018	KC	6603	-6.4	0.0	-0.2	-6.7
2019	COL	1969	-1.3	1.2	0.0	-0.1
2020	COL	1958	0.0	0.1	0.0	0.1
2021	TEX	16650	-9.9	3.5	0.4	-6.0
2021	TEX	16650	-9.9	3.2	0.4	-6.4

YEAR	TEAM	LVL	AGE	PA	DRC+	BABIP	BRR	FRAA	WARP
2018	KC	MLB	34	166	79	.232	1.2	C(48): -6.9, 1B(2): 0.9, P(1): -0.0	-0.1
2018	COL	MLB	34	16	78	.182	0.1	C(6): -0.9, 1B(4): 0.0	-0.1
2019	ABQ	AAA	35	262	108	.356	0.3	C(65): -5.7	1.1
2019	COL	MLB	35	49	62	.233	0.5	C(14): 0.2, 1B(3): 0.0	0.1
2020	COL	MLB	36	43	75	.207	-0.3	C(25): -0.2, 1B(5): -0.1, P(1): 0.2	0.0
2021 FS	TEX	MLB	37	600	59	.263	-0.5	C -6, 1B 0	-1.4

Justin Foscue 2B

Born: 03/02/99 Age: 22 Bats: R Throws: R
Height: 6'0" Weight: 203 Origin: Round 1, 2020 Draft (#14 overall)

It was a bit of a surprise when the Rangers nabbed Justin Foscue out of Mississippi State with the 14th pick in the 2020 MLB Draft, but the infielder offers a fairly high floor at the plate, blending a solid hit tool with above-average plate discipline. The Rangers have made it clear that longtime second baseman Rougned Odor won't stand as an obstacle, so Foscue is slated to man the keystone for now, with third base also a possibility. His big-league upside will depend on how much the power he demonstrated in college will translate.

Texas Rangers 2021

Ronald Guzmán 1B

Born: 10/20/94   Age: 26   Bats: L   Throws: L
Height: 6'5"   Weight: 235   Origin: International Free Agent, 2011

YEAR	TEAM	LVL	AGE	PA	R	2B	3B	HR	RBI	BB	K	SB	CS	AVG/OBP/SLG
2018	TEX	MLB	23	428	46	18	2	16	58	33	121	1	0	.235/.306/.416
2019	NAS	AAA	24	135	22	8	0	5	16	17	31	0	0	.308/.400/.504
2019	TEX	MLB	24	295	34	20	0	10	36	32	87	1	2	.219/.308/.414
2020	TEX	MLB	25	86	10	1	1	4	9	7	24	1	0	.244/.314/.436
2021 FS	TEX	MLB	26	600	69	25	2	22	70	51	171	0	1	.235/.310/.415
2021 DC	TEX	MLB	26	155	17	6	0	5	18	13	44	0	0	.235/.310/.415

Comparables: Derrek Lee, Bob Chance, Ron Jackson

It's awfully tough to be a 1B-only prospect, especially when you're a 1B-only prospect who doesn't hit for a lot of power. There was a time when Guzman was considered an interesting, if not exciting, prospect, as he doubled his way up the ladder. Upon being thrust into big-league action, Guzman didn't hit much, but he did flash the leather, wowing with uncanny stretches at the cold corner. The novelty and newness was exciting. Fast forward to 2020 and the offense remains as middling as ever and the defense is slipping, calling into question Guzman's usefulness. In fact, perhaps the most intriguing part of Guzman's early career has been his allegiance to animal welfare, with him adopting a condor, his nickname-sake, and naming the bird "Guzzy". While The Condor adopting a condor is a heartwarming story, Guzman will have to soar at the plate in the very near future if he doesn't want to meet the same fate as his feathery friend, flirting with the endangered species list.

YEAR	TEAM	LVL	AGE	PA	DRC+	BABIP	BRR	FRAA	WARP
2018	TEX	MLB	23	428	91	.299	1.9	1B(117): 1.9	0.6
2019	NAS	AAA	24	135	113	.383	-1.3	1B(23): 0.5	0.3
2019	TEX	MLB	24	295	85	.282	-2.5	1B(81): 6.2	0.3
2020	TEX	MLB	25	86	89	.300	0.0	1B(24): 2.0	0.2
2021 FS	TEX	MLB	26	600	93	.305	-0.6	1B 1	0.4
2021 DC	TEX	MLB	26	155	93	.305	-0.2	1B 0	0.1

Jonah Heim C

Born: 06/27/95 Age: 26 Bats: S Throws: R
Height: 6'4" Weight: 220 Origin: Round 4, 2013 Draft (#129 overall)

YEAR	TEAM	LVL	AGE	PA	R	2B	3B	HR	RBI	BB	K	SB	CS	AVG/OBP/SLG
2018	STK	HI-A	23	348	41	21	1	7	49	29	60	3	1	.292/.353/.433
2018	MID	AA	23	154	16	4	0	1	11	10	22	0	0	.182/.238/.234
2019	MID	AA	24	208	20	12	0	5	34	24	27	0	1	.282/.370/.431
2019	LV	AAA	24	119	22	9	0	4	19	11	18	0	0	.358/.412/.557
2020	OAK	MLB	25	41	5	0	0	0	5	3	3	0	0	.211/.268/.211
2021 FS	TEX	MLB	26	600	63	24	1	14	59	45	124	0	0	.225/.289/.355
2021 DC	TEX	MLB	26	60	6	2	0	1	5	4	12	0	0	.225/.289/.355

Comparables: Sandy León, Jose Reyes, Steven Lerud

The Battle of Helm's Deep, the climax of Peter Jackson's adaptation of *The Two Towers*, is one of the most revered and complex battle scenes ever put to film—it was shot over four months (mostly during the night) and utilized a 1:4 scale miniature that still spanned 50 feet long. The battle for Heim, depth, was less epic in scale—midway through the season, the seven-year minors veteran (on his third organization) got the call to replace Austin Allen as the A's backup. The defense is better-regarded in Heim's case than Allen's, but backup has long appeared the top of the scale—even if you forgive the disastrous first shot at Double-A in 2018, a solid eye in the box is the only notable offensive tool. The battle for a backup role nevertheless ended in a decisive win for Heim—he got rostered for the playoffs, though he didn't appear.

YEAR	TEAM	P. COUNT	FRM RUNS	BLK RUNS	THRW RUNS	TOT RUNS
2019	LV	3229	1.1	0.0	0.2	1.3
2020	OAK	1456	0.0	0.0	0.0	-0.1
2021	TEX	16650	0.8	1.5	0.2	2.5
2021	TEX	16650	0.8	1.5	0.2	2.5

YEAR	TEAM	LVL	AGE	PA	DRC+	BABIP	BRR	FRAA	WARP
2018	STK	HI-A	23	348	117	.337	-0.9	C(55): -0.1	0.8
2018	MID	AA	23	154	22	.205	-0.9	C(38): 1.6	-0.8
2019	MID	AA	24	208	137	.307	-1.6	C(43): 7.7	2.3
2019	LV	AAA	24	119	124	.395	-0.5	C(28): 2.2	1.0
2020	OAK	MLB	25	41	94	.229	-0.1	C(12): 0.3	0.2
2021 FS	TEX	MLB	26	600	74	.268	-0.9	C 2	0.6
2021 DC	TEX	MLB	26	60	74	.268	-0.1	C 3	0.3

Texas Rangers 2021

Sam Huff C

Born: 01/14/98   Age: 23   Bats: R   Throws: R
Height: 6'5"   Weight: 240   Origin: Round 7, 2016 Draft (#219 overall)

YEAR	TEAM	LVL	AGE	PA	R	2B	3B	HR	RBI	BB	K	SB	CS	AVG/OBP/SLG
2018	HIC	LO-A	20	448	53	22	3	18	55	23	140	9	1	.241/.292/.439
2019	HIC	LO-A	21	114	22	5	0	15	29	6	37	4	1	.333/.368/.796
2019	DE	HI-A	21	405	49	17	2	13	43	27	117	2	5	.262/.326/.425
2020	TEX	MLB	22	33	5	3	0	3	4	2	11	0	0	.355/.394/.742
2021 FS	TEX	MLB	23	600	64	25	2	17	64	40	228	2	2	.208/.271/.358
2021 DC	TEX	MLB	23	216	23	9	0	6	23	14	82	0	1	.208/.271/.358

Comparables: Jorge Alfaro, Eric Haase, Tommy Joseph

In the history of Major League Baseball, just four catchers (Joe Mauer, Matt Wieters, Sandy Alomar, Jr., and Larry McLean) have eclipsed Huff's 6'4" frame. He also hits the ball in keeping with his stature: Had Huff

YEAR	TEAM	P. COUNT	FRM RUNS	BLK RUNS	THRW RUNS	TOT RUNS
2020	TEX	1459	-0.6	0.0	0.0	-0.6
2021	TEX	8418	-3.6	1.3	0.1	-2.2
2021	TEX	8418	-3.6	0.4	0.1	-3.1

qualified, only Fernando Tatis, Jr. would have posted a higher percentage of hard hit balls, which is decent company to keep. The 2020 success at the plate will likely regress some, as can be expected from a guy that jumped to the big leagues without experience above High-A. Still, three dingers in his first 10 games as a big leaguer is a decent start, and the bar on offense behind the plate is so low these days that, even with regression, Huff has the chance to be an excellent offensive catcher. How about the defense, you ask? Well, he's not a disaster or a liability, which isn't exactly a ringing endorsement, but it'll allow him to start most days of the week.

YEAR	TEAM	LVL	AGE	PA	DRC+	BABIP	BRR	FRAA	WARP
2018	HIC	LO-A	20	448	96	.317	-0.1	C(56): 1.9, 1B(11): -0.4	0.4
2019	HIC	LO-A	21	114	216	.375	0.8	C(14): 0.9	1.8
2019	DE	HI-A	21	405	110	.347	-2.7	C(51): 1.9, 1B(4): 0.1	1.5
2020	TEX	MLB	22	33	103	.471	-0.8	C(10): 0.1	0.0
2021 FS	TEX	MLB	23	600	69	.319	-0.5	C -4, 1B 0	-0.5
2021 DC	TEX	MLB	23	216	69	.319	-0.2	C -2	-0.2

Josh Jung   3B

Born: 02/12/98   Age: 23   Bats: R   Throws: R
Height: 6'2"   Weight: 215   Origin: Round 1, 2019 Draft (#8 overall)

YEAR	TEAM	LVL	AGE	PA	R	2B	3B	HR	RBI	BB	K	SB	CS	AVG/OBP/SLG
2019	RAN	ROK	21	19	5	1	1	1	5	2	3	0	0	.588/.632/.941
2019	HIC	LO-A	21	179	18	13	0	1	23	16	29	4	1	.287/.363/.389
2021 FS	TEX	MLB	23	600	58	24	2	8	52	36	157	2	2	.220/.278/.318
2021 DC	TEX	MLB	23	166	16	6	0	2	14	10	43	0	1	.220/.278/.318

Comparables: Garin Cecchini, Jedd Gyorko, Stephen Piscotty

Jung was born in San Antonio, TX, where he'd later go to high school. He went to Texas Tech for college, and was drafted in the first round by the Texas Rangers. As the great American poet, Tim Riggins, once said: "Texas, forever". Despite being a clear fish out of water in High-A Hickory (in North Carolina, can you *imagine*?), Jung still displayed his personal blend of high-contact offense with above-average defense. He should be more comfortable back in Texas at Double-A Frisco, where he's likely to start next season, and manager Chris Woodward has already hinted at the likelihood of Jung manning the hot corner in Arlington at some point during the 2021 campaign. His long-term power output will likely depend on whether some of his all-field approach turns into pull-side dingers, but there's definitely pop in Jung's bat, and there's plenty of time for him to figure out what kind of player he'll be. If everything's bigger in Texas, Jung's prospect hype train should shortly follow suit.

YEAR	TEAM	LVL	AGE	PA	DRC+	BABIP	BRR	FRAA	WARP
2019	RAN	ROK	21	19		.692			
2019	HIC	LO-A	21	179	136	.341	0.6	3B(35): 2.5	1.5
2021 FS	TEX	MLB	23	600	64	.295	-0.4	3B 15	-0.2
2021 DC	TEX	MLB	23	166	64	.295	-0.1	3B 4	0.0

Bayron Lora RF

Born: 09/29/02   Age: 18   Bats: R   Throws: R
Height: 6'3"   Weight: 190   Origin: International Free Agent, 2019

You might not know a lot about Lora, the enormous teenager that signed for a cool $4 million in the 2019 J2 signing period, and that's okay. For serious baseball card collectors, though, Lora has been a hot name in 2020, with his Bowman Chrome autograph card fetching upwards of $4,000 at online retailers. Gone are the days of putting cards in your bicycle spokes, apparently. While that lofty price tag seems a little premature, Lora is an awfully exciting prospect, possessing light-tower power and displaying decent athleticism for his advanced size at a non-advanced age. You could say that card collectors are taking the same risk that the Rangers took—putting a down payment on a dude that has the ability to out-earn the initial investment.

Nate Lowe 1B

Born: 07/07/95   Age: 26   Bats: L   Throws: R
Height: 6'4"   Weight: 220   Origin: Round 13, 2016 Draft (#390 overall)

YEAR	TEAM	LVL	AGE	PA	R	2B	3B	HR	RBI	BB	K	SB	CS	AVG/OBP/SLG
2018	CHA	HI-A	22	220	39	15	0	10	44	25	33	0	0	.356/.432/.588
2018	MTG	AA	22	225	36	11	0	13	42	35	30	1	1	.340/.444/.606
2018	DUR	AAA	22	110	18	6	1	4	16	8	27	0	0	.260/.327/.460
2019	DUR	AAA	23	406	63	24	0	16	63	72	82	1	0	.289/.421/.508
2019	TB	MLB	23	169	24	8	0	7	19	13	50	0	0	.263/.325/.454
2020	TB	MLB	24	76	10	2	0	4	11	9	28	1	0	.224/.316/.433
2021 FS	TEX	MLB	25	600	76	26	1	24	72	69	181	0	0	.241/.336/.433
2021 DC	TEX	MLB	25	499	63	22	1	20	60	57	151	0	0	.241/.336/.433

Comparables: Tony Clark, Brad Eldred, Carlos Delgado

The Rangers, who had been chasing Lowe for a while, caught him last winter as part of the winter's most boring six-player trade. He's been a slightly above-average hitter in 245 big-league plate appearances, but the Rays never seem compelled to give him an extended look. The rebuilding Rangers, on the other hand, have every reason to see if Lowe can walk-and-bop enough to serve as their first baseman of the present and the future.

YEAR	TEAM	LVL	AGE	PA	DRC+	BABIP	BRR	FRAA	WARP
2018	CHA	HI-A	22	220	207	.391	-2.4	1B(35): -2.9	1.7
2018	MTG	AA	22	225	211	.349	1.9	1B(39): -0.4	2.7
2018	DUR	AAA	22	110	116	.319	-1.2	1B(25): -0.1	0.0
2019	DUR	AAA	23	406	142	.341	-0.6	1B(72): -1.0, 3B(5): 0.3	2.3
2019	TB	MLB	23	169	88	.340	1.0	1B(21): 0.1, 3B(4): -0.2	0.1
2020	TB	MLB	24	76	85	.314	-0.3	1B(15): -0.6, 3B(2): -0.1	-0.1
2021 FS	TEX	MLB	25	600	106	.324	-0.9	1B 0, 3B -1	1.2
2021 DC	TEX	MLB	25	499	106	.324	-0.8	1B 0, 3B 0	1.0

Danny Santana OF

Born: 11/07/90 Age: 30 Bats: S Throws: R
Height: 5'11" Weight: 195 Origin: International Free Agent, 2007

YEAR	TEAM	LVL	AGE	PA	R	2B	3B	HR	RBI	BB	K	SB	CS	AVG/OBP/SLG
2018	GWN	AAA	27	342	57	21	3	16	40	15	80	12	5	.264/.294/.497
2018	ATL	MLB	27	32	4	3	0	0	2	3	11	1	1	.179/.281/.286
2019	NAS	AAA	28	40	4	4	1	0	6	4	10	1	1	.343/.425/.514
2019	TEX	MLB	28	511	81	23	6	28	81	25	151	21	6	.283/.324/.534
2020	TEX	MLB	29	63	6	4	0	1	7	7	24	2	0	.145/.238/.273
2021 FS	TEX	MLB	30	600	61	28	3	21	72	32	185	18	7	.226/.276/.403

Comparables: Randy Kutcher, Corey Patterson, Carlos Gómez

Who built Stonehenge? What happened to Amelia Earhart? Why did someone think Rocky V would be a good idea? History is chock full of great mysteries, but perhaps none greater than this: What in the hell was up with Danny Santana in 2019? After bouncing around in a few MLB organizations, Santana signed a minor-league deal with the Rangers and proceeded to post career-high offensive numbers, including 28 homers—more than double his cumulative career total to that point. Then came the Great Regression. Santana got just one hit in his first 17 trips to the plate to kick off the season, battling injuries and flat-out poor performance until a balky elbow ended his season for good. In September, he underwent a modified Tommy John surgery, where an internal brace was used to repair and connect ligaments as opposed to human tendons. In theory, the switch-hitter could be back in Arlington in March 2021, but whether or not he'll 1) recover from the innovative procedure or 2) reclaim his form and spot in the lineup lies hidden in the shroud of the future.

YEAR	TEAM	LVL	AGE	PA	DRC+	BABIP	BRR	FRAA	WARP
2018	GWN	AAA	27	342	103	.301	1.5	CF(45): 1.1, 2B(14): 1.3, LF(9): 3.0	1.3
2018	ATL	MLB	27	32	70	.294	-0.7	LF(6): 0.1, CF(3): -0.1, RF(1): -0.1	-0.1
2019	NAS	AAA	28	40	117	.480	1.1	SS(3): 0.8, RF(3): -0.2, 2B(1): 0.1	0.3
2019	TEX	MLB	28	511	106	.353	3.6	1B(44): 0.9, CF(27): 0.6, 2B(17): 0.8	2.1
2020	TEX	MLB	29	63	69	.226	0.3	1B(9): -0.6, CF(4): 0.9, LF(1): -0.0	-0.1
2021 FS	TEX	MLB	30	600	78	.299	1.9	CF 1, 1B 0	0.3

Bubba Thompson OF

Born: 06/09/98 Age: 23 Bats: R Throws: R
Height: 6'1" Weight: 180 Origin: Round 1, 2017 Draft (#26 overall)

YEAR	TEAM	LVL	AGE	PA	R	2B	3B	HR	RBI	BB	K	SB	CS	AVG/OBP/SLG
2018	HIC	LO-A	20	363	52	18	5	8	42	23	104	32	7	.289/.344/.446
2019	DE	HI-A	21	228	24	8	2	5	21	21	72	12	3	.178/.261/.312
2021 FS	*TEX*	*MLB*	*23*	*600*	*46*	*21*	*3*	*10*	*52*	*33*	*224*	*19*	*8*	*.189/.243/.300*

Comparables: Bubba Starling, Daz Cameron, Tommy Pham

If you bet that a dude named Bubba Thompson was someone SEC schools would be falling all over themselves to recruit, well, you'd be right. Tennessee and Mississippi both wanted him to play quarterback. Auburn thought they had secured Thompson's talents only for him to commit to Alabama, a reverse Kick Six, in a sense. Of course, it all was moot in the end, as Thompson signed with the Rangers before enrolling in classes. In the time since, the outfielder has surged up Texas' organizational rankings, blending the type of athleticism that made offensive coordinators salivate and the speed and ability to make hard contact that got him drafted in the first round. Thompson has definitely missed his fair share of time since the start of the 2019 campaign, so there will likely be plenty of rust to shake off. Having said that, it wasn't long ago when he was considered one of the better prospects in the game, and potentially the long-term future in center field.

YEAR	TEAM	LVL	AGE	PA	DRC+	BABIP	BRR	FRAA	WARP
2018	HIC	LO-A	20	363	117	.396	6.1	CF(67): 1.1, LF(17): 0.7	1.9
2019	DE	HI-A	21	228	54	.246	2.6	LF(34): 1.5, CF(20): -1.8, RF(2): -0.3	-0.2
2021 FS	*TEX*	*MLB*	*23*	*600*	*46*	*.293*	*2.3*	*CF 1, LF 5*	*-1.5*

Steele Walker CF

Born: 07/30/96   Age: 24   Bats: L   Throws: L
Height: 5'11"   Weight: 190   Origin: Round 2, 2018 Draft (#46 overall)

YEAR	TEAM	LVL	AGE	PA	R	2B	3B	HR	RBI	BB	K	SB	CS	AVG/OBP/SLG
2018	WSX	ROK	21	13	0	0	0	0	0	1	1	0	0	.455/.538/.455
2018	GTF	ROK	21	38	4	1	0	2	4	1	7	1	1	.206/.263/.412
2018	KAN	LO-A	21	126	13	5	0	3	17	8	29	5	1	.186/.246/.310
2019	KAN	LO-A	22	87	6	10	3	0	11	8	15	4	2	.365/.437/.581
2019	WS	HI-A	22	441	59	26	2	10	51	42	63	9	5	.269/.346/.426
2021 FS	TEX	MLB	24	600	54	28	2	13	60	35	151	5	3	.223/.281/.356

Comparables: Lastings Milledge, Charlie Blackmon, Matt Szczur

Though 2020 was mostly a lost development year for Walker, the joy his trade to the Rangers brought to Twitter users dying to make puns about 90s syndicated television justified the cost. Less obvious, but equally vital information: His name doubles as something you should never do when visiting a nursing home.

YEAR	TEAM	LVL	AGE	PA	DRC+	BABIP	BRR	FRAA	WARP
2018	WSX	ROK	21	13		.500			
2018	GTF	ROK	21	38		.192			
2018	KAN	LO-A	21	126	57	.214	0.3	CF(21): 1.2	-0.3
2019	KAN	LO-A	22	87	179	.443	-0.4	CF(16): -1.7, RF(4): -0.1	0.6
2019	WS	HI-A	22	441	126	.294	-1.0	CF(81): -2.5	2.0
2021 FS	TEX	MLB	24	600	72	.286	-0.1	CF 4, RF 0	0.1

Eli White LF

Born: 06/26/94   Age: 27   Bats: R   Throws: R
Height: 6'3"   Weight: 195   Origin: Round 11, 2016 Draft (#322 overall)

YEAR	TEAM	LVL	AGE	PA	R	2B	3B	HR	RBI	BB	K	SB	CS	AVG/OBP/SLG
2018	MID	AA	24	578	81	30	8	9	55	62	116	18	9	.306/.388/.450
2019	NAS	AAA	25	499	63	20	5	14	43	43	136	14	5	.253/.337/.418
2020	TEX	MLB	26	52	5	2	0	0	3	3	16	1	1	.188/.231/.229
2021 FS	TEX	MLB	27	600	63	24	3	13	57	46	190	5	3	.221/.295/.351
2021 DC	TEX	MLB	27	150	15	6	0	3	14	11	47	1	1	.221/.295/.351

Comparables: Brandon Hicks, José Rondón, Tim Beckham

In *The Book of Eli*, a blind Denzel Washington treks across a post-apocalyptic United States on foot, in an attempt to preserve culture by delivering the last remaining copy of the Bible to Alcatraz. Eli White trekked from Oakland to Arlington, after being swapped for Jurickson Profar, in an attempt to preserve the organization's positional flexibility. Though he made his big-league debut in the outfield, White played up the middle on the dirt as a minor leaguer, providing serviceable, if not better, defense to blend with his "little bit of power/little bit of speed" profile at the plate. The book *on* Eli is breaking balls. Lots and lots of breaking balls. Breaking balls early and breaking balls often.

YEAR	TEAM	LVL	AGE	PA	DRC+	BABIP	BRR	FRAA	WARP
2018	MID	AA	24	578	132	.379	3.2	2B(66): 2.8, SS(42): 2.6, 3B(19): -1.4	3.3
2019	NAS	AAA	25	499	79	.333	1.7	SS(92): -6.8, CF(22): -0.5, 2B(2): 0.0	0.6
2020	TEX	MLB	26	52	73	.273	-0.6	LF(13): -1.5, RF(3): -0.1, CF(1): -0.2	-0.2
2021 FS	TEX	MLB	27	600	75	.318	0.1	SS -1, RF -1	-0.4
2021 DC	TEX	MLB	27	150	75	.318	0.0	SS 0, RF 0	-0.1

Justin Anderson RHP

Born: 09/28/92   Age: 28   Bats: L   Throws: R
Height: 6'3"   Weight: 230   Origin: Round 14, 2014 Draft (#419 overall)

YEAR	TEAM	LVL	AGE	W	L	SV	G	GS	IP	H	HR	BB/9	K/9	K	GB%	BABIP
2018	SL	AAA	25	0	0	0	3	0	5	0	0	1.8	10.8	6	77.8%	.000
2018	LAA	MLB	25	3	3	4	57	0	55[1]	42	3	6.5	10.9	67	52.7%	.310
2019	LAA	MLB	26	3	0	1	54	0	47	42	6	6.1	11.5	60	34.7%	.308
2021 FS	TEX	MLB	28	2	2	0	57	0	50	42	7	5.5	10.2	56	42.3%	.285

Comparables: Kyle Crick, Sam Tuivailala, Dovydas Neverauskas

Speaking about his feelings about undergoing Tommy John surgery—after an injury on his first pitch in an intrasquad game—Anderson said, "It's an issue you think won't ever happen." He must have been watching a different Angels squad the past half-decade. Having surgery in July means it's tenuous to expect Anderson to appear in 2021.

YEAR	TEAM	LVL	AGE	WHIP	ERA	DRA-	WARP	MPH	FB%	WHF	CSP
2018	SL	AAA	25	0.20	0.00	78	0.1				
2018	LAA	MLB	25	1.48	4.07	101	0.3	99.1	44.9%	37.2%	
2019	LAA	MLB	26	1.57	5.55	99	0.3	96.0	47.1%	28.0%	
2021 FS	TEX	MLB	28	1.47	4.57	100	0.2	97.1	46.3%	31.4%	42.2%

Kohei Arihara RHP
Born: 08/11/92 Age: 28 Bats: R Throws: R
Height: 6'2" Weight: 210 Origin: International Free Agent, 2020

YEAR	TEAM	LVL	AGE	W	L	SV	G	GS	IP	H	HR	BB/9	K/9	K	GB%	BABIP
2021 FS	TEX	MLB	28	2	2	0	57	0	50	49	7	2.5	7.3	40	40.7%	.288
2021 DC	TEX	MLB	28	9	7	0	25	25	139.7	137	21	2.5	7.3	113	40.7%	.288

    Waseda University, whose storied baseball program predates the Yomiuri Giants, the oldest professional club in Japan, has produced three major leaguers: Satoru Komiya, Nori Aoki, and Tsuyoshi Wada. In 2021, Arihara is set to become the fourth. Unlike his rubber-toeing predecessors, the right-hander gets to test himself before he turns 30, with health and prime stuff, including a low-90s fastball and a low-80s changeup, seemingly intact. While Arihara doesn't possess the upside of the last two hurlers posted by Nippon Ham—Yu Darvish and Shohei Ohtani—he is capable of serving as an adequate mid-rotation starter in the major leagues.

YEAR	TEAM	LVL	AGE	WHIP	ERA	DRA-	WARP	MPH	FB%	WHF	CSP
2021 FS	TEX	MLB	28	1.26	3.90	94	0.4				
2021 DC	TEX	MLB	28	1.26	3.90	94	1.8				

Zack Brown RHP

Born: 12/15/94 Age: 26 Bats: R Throws: R
Height: 6'1" Weight: 199 Origin: Round 5, 2016 Draft (#141 overall)

YEAR	TEAM	LVL	AGE	W	L	SV	G	GS	IP	H	HR	BB/9	K/9	K	GB%	BABIP
2018	BRG	ROK	23	0	0	0	1	1	2	3	0	4.5	13.5	3	16.7%	.500
2018	BLX	AA	23	9	1	0	22	21	125^2	95	8	2.6	8.3	116	55.5%	.258
2019	SA	AAA	24	3	7	0	25	23	116^2	138	16	4.9	7.6	98	52.3%	.349
2021 FS	TEX	MLB	26	2	2	0	57	0	50	46	7	4.1	7.6	42	50.5%	.274

Comparables: Erik Johnson, Ryan Helsley, Nabil Crismatt

Few pitchers make any kind of lasting mark in the majors after twice being left unprotected in the Rule 5 Draft. That said, Brown is better than almost anyone who meets that criterion. The Brewers' organizational philosophy about such decisions is one of the most aggressive in the majors, and since Brown had no opportunity to bounce back from a poor 2019 in competitive 2020 contests, the team rolled the dice to keep an extra spot on their 40-man roster. He did, by most accounts, have a productive summer at the club's alternate site, but that didn't answer the questions about his confidence or ability to throw strikes that cropped up in 2019. With a delivery long on effort and short on early stability, Brown doesn't project to develop starter-caliber control, and his stuff might tick up if he moves to the bullpen.

YEAR	TEAM	LVL	AGE	WHIP	ERA	DRA-	WARP	MPH	FB%	WHF	CSP
2018	BRG	ROK	23	2.00	0.00						
2018	BLX	AA	23	1.04	2.44	72	2.8				
2019	SA	AAA	24	1.73	5.79	134	0.2				
2021 FS	TEX	MLB	26	1.40	4.48	103	0.2				

Brock Burke LHP

Born: 08/04/96 Age: 24 Bats: L Throws: L
Height: 6'4" Weight: 210 Origin: Round 3, 2014 Draft (#96 overall)

YEAR	TEAM	LVL	AGE	W	L	SV	G	GS	IP	H	HR	BB/9	K/9	K	GB%	BABIP
2018	CHA	HI-A	21	3	5	0	16	13	82	85	4	3.3	9.5	87	45.4%	.349
2018	MTG	AA	21	6	1	0	9	9	55^1	39	2	2.3	11.5	71	35.3%	.285
2019	FRI	AA	22	3	5	0	9	9	45^1	34	2	2.4	9.7	49	47.5%	.271
2019	NAS	AAA	22	0	0	0	2	2	8	12	1	6.8	12.4	11	50.0%	.478
2019	TEX	MLB	22	0	2	0	6	6	26^2	30	6	3.7	4.7	14	48.4%	.279
2021 FS	TEX	MLB	24	2	2	0	57	0	50	49	6	3.7	7.8	43	44.2%	.299
2021 DC	TEX	MLB	24	1	1	0	23	0	24.7	24	3	3.7	7.8	21	44.2%	.299

Comparables: Pedro Avila, Logan Allen, Patrick Sandoval

In Greek mythology, Sisyphus was tasked with forever rolling a giant boulder up a hill, only for it to roll back down whenever he got close to the top. Burke debuted in the big leagues in 2019, logging three consecutive quality starts in his first three outings. From there, well, the boulder got a little creaky. In his next three starts, Burke made it through a combined 8⅔ innings, giving up 19 earned runs, and serving up six dingers before a shoulder impingement shuttered the rest of his season. The injury wasn't thought to be serious, but it did delay the southpaw's start to the 2020 campaign. Then, while ramping up, Burke was diagnosed with a torn labrum, succumbing to surgery and requiring 12 months of rehab. And just like that, the boulder had returned to its original resting place. He'll start pushing it back up the hill starting in March 2021, hopefully with different results.

YEAR	TEAM	LVL	AGE	WHIP	ERA	DRA-	WARP	MPH	FB%	WHF	CSP
2018	CHA	HI-A	21	1.40	3.84	82	1.2				
2018	MTG	AA	21	0.96	1.95	68	1.3				
2019	FRI	AA	22	1.01	3.18	56	1.2				
2019	NAS	AAA	22	2.25	7.88	138	0.0				
2019	TEX	MLB	22	1.54	7.42	139	-0.3	94.2	61.3%	13.1%	
2021 FS	TEX	MLB	24	1.41	4.45	102	0.2	94.2	61.3%	13.1%	50.5%
2021 DC	TEX	MLB	24	1.41	4.45	102	0.2	94.2	61.3%	13.1%	50.5%

Hans Crouse RHP

Born: 09/15/98   Age: 22   Bats: L   Throws: R
Height: 6'4"   Weight: 180   Origin: Round 2, 2017 Draft (#66 overall)

YEAR	TEAM	LVL	AGE	W	L	SV	G	GS	IP	H	HR	BB/9	K/9	K	GB%	BABIP
2018	SPO	SS	19	5	1	0	8	8	38	25	2	2.6	11.1	47	35.5%	.253
2018	HIC	LO-A	19	0	2	0	5	5	16^2	18	1	4.3	8.1	15	38.5%	.340
2019	HIC	LO-A	20	6	1	0	19	19	87^2	86	12	2.0	7.7	75	31.3%	.295
2021 FS	TEX	MLB	22	2	3	0	57	0	50	48	8	4.0	8.0	44	32.7%	.286

Comparables: Joe Ross, Robert Gsellman, Felix Doubront

A fun way to spend the winter months is to compile a thorough, definitive list of the greatest Hanses of history. It's a time-honored tradition. Hans Gruber, the greatest movie villain of all time, is number one. Apologies to fans of Hans Geiger, the inventor of the Geiger counter, as his measurement of radiation brings him just short (ranked number six). Hans Christian Anderson ranks highly for his beloved fairy tales, but perhaps not as high as you'd think (number nine), and while Hans, of the famed comedy duo Hans and Franz, is good for a chuckle, his schtick gets old quickly (number 54). Hans Zimmer is responsible for some of the greatest modern movie scores and that's good enough to get him just outside the top-10 (number 11). Hans-Ulrich Rudel is last. Where Crouse slots in is still to be decided. He's got the size and two plus pitches, which bodes well for his tenure in the rotation, but unfortunately he also has the spotty command and violent delivery of a relief risk. A third pitch and improved precision will go a long way to determining whether Crouse is closer to Hans Holzer, Austrian-American author, parapsychologist, and host of the television show Ghost Hunters (number 13) or Hans, the late skate-shop owner from Mighty Ducks (number 35).

YEAR	TEAM	LVL	AGE	WHIP	ERA	DRA-	WARP	MPH	FB%	WHF	CSP
2018	SPO	SS	19	0.95	2.37	91	0.4				
2018	HIC	LO-A	19	1.56	2.70	135	-0.2				
2019	HIC	LO-A	20	1.20	4.41	105	0.1				
2021 FS	TEX	MLB	22	1.42	4.68	110	0.0				

Demarcus Evans RHP

Born: 10/22/96   Age: 24   Bats: R   Throws: R
Height: 6'5"   Weight: 265   Origin: Round 25, 2015 Draft (#738 overall)

YEAR	TEAM	LVL	AGE	W	L	SV	G	GS	IP	H	HR	BB/9	K/9	K	GB%	BABIP
2018	HIC	LO-A	21	4	1	9	35	0	56	28	1	4.3	16.6	103	34.8%	.314
2019	DE	HI-A	22	4	0	6	17	0	22^1	9	0	6.9	16.1	40	45.5%	.290
2019	FRI	AA	22	2	0	6	30	0	37^2	14	2	5.3	14.3	60	34.9%	.197
2020	TEX	MLB	23	0	0	0	4	0	4	3	1	0.0	9.0	4	33.3%	.250
2021 FS	TEX	MLB	24	2	2	0	57	0	50	40	6	6.8	13.0	72	37.0%	.315
2021 DC	TEX	MLB	24	2	2	0	53	0	55.3	45	7	6.8	13.0	79	37.0%	.315

Comparables: Cristian Javier, Carlos Sanabria, Carlos Estévez

The first batter Evans faced in his big-league career was Albert Pujols, who promptly welcomed the righty to The Show with a homer. The rest of the league welcomed him much more politely, thanks to his heavy 95 mph heater and wipeout curve that induces a ton of whiffs.

YEAR	TEAM	LVL	AGE	WHIP	ERA	DRA-	WARP	MPH	FB%	WHF	CSP
2018	HIC	LO-A	21	0.98	1.77	56	1.4				
2019	DE	HI-A	22	1.16	0.81	62	0.4				
2019	FRI	AA	22	0.96	0.96	48	1.0				
2020	TEX	MLB	23	0.75	2.25	100	0.0	95.5	66.7%	29.6%	
2021 FS	TEX	MLB	24	1.57	4.74	103	0.2	95.5	66.7%	29.6%	40.6%
2021 DC	TEX	MLB	24	1.57	4.74	103	0.2	95.5	66.7%	29.6%	40.6%

Mike Foltynewicz   RHP
Born: 10/07/91   Age: 29   Bats: R   Throws: R
Height: 6'4"   Weight: 195   Origin: Round 1, 2010 Draft (#19 overall)

YEAR	TEAM	LVL	AGE	W	L	SV	G	GS	IP	H	HR	BB/9	K/9	K	GB%	BABIP
2018	ATL	MLB	26	13	10	0	31	31	183	130	17	3.3	9.9	202	43.0%	.252
2019	GWN	AAA	27	5	1	0	10	10	51¹	49	1	3.0	7.9	45	39.2%	.318
2019	ATL	MLB	27	8	6	0	21	21	117	109	23	2.8	8.1	105	36.9%	.270
2020	ATL	MLB	28	0	1	0	1	1	3¹	4	3	10.8	8.1	3	44.4%	.167
2021 FS	TEX	MLB	29	2	2	0	57	0	50	47	8	3.4	8.6	47	39.0%	.289
2021 DC	TEX	MLB	29	7	7	0	22	22	117.7	111	19	3.4	8.6	112	39.0%	.289

Comparables: Kevin Gausman, Trevor Williams, Jon Gray

  On October 4, 2019, Foltynewicz shut out the Cardinals over seven innings, striking out seven, to win Game 2 of the NLDS. After that date, he was obliterated in that series' Game 5, giving up seven runs in the first inning; was hit hard in spring training and then again in summer camp; made all of one 2020 start in which he was hammered for six runs in 3⅓ innings and struggled to crack 90 mph with a fastball that once averaged 96 and was subsequently designated for assignment and banished to the Braves' alternate site. There he spent the remainder of the season, watching as his team traded for Tommy Milone for rotation help. Life, as the saying goes, comes at you fast, and in Foltynewicz's case, it ran into him like a freight train going light speed. Where he goes from here is anyone's guess.

YEAR	TEAM	LVL	AGE	WHIP	ERA	DRA-	WARP	MPH	FB%	WHF	CSP
2018	ATL	MLB	26	1.08	2.85	76	3.9	98.6	56.3%	25.4%	
2019	GWN	AAA	27	1.29	3.86	75	1.5				
2019	ATL	MLB	27	1.25	4.54	89	1.8	97.3	52.2%	23.5%	
2020	ATL	MLB	28	2.40	16.20	138	0.0	92.5	44.3%	14.3%	
2021 FS	TEX	MLB	29	1.32	4.20	98	0.3	97.7	53.7%	24.1%	49.8%
2021 DC	TEX	MLB	29	1.32	4.20	98	1.3	97.7	53.7%	24.1%	49.8%

José Leclerc RHP
Born: 12/19/93   Age: 27   Bats: R   Throws: R
Height: 6'0"   Weight: 195   Origin: International Free Agent, 2010

YEAR	TEAM	LVL	AGE	W	L	SV	G	GS	IP	H	HR	BB/9	K/9	K	GB%	BABIP
2018	TEX	MLB	24	2	3	12	59	0	57²	24	1	3.9	13.1	84	30.9%	.217
2019	TEX	MLB	25	2	4	14	70	3	68²	52	7	5.1	13.1	100	34.4%	.312
2020	TEX	MLB	26	0	0	1	2	0	2	2	0	9.0	13.5	3	0.0%	.400
2021 FS	TEX	MLB	27	2	2	20	57	0	50	37	6	6.1	12.7	70	34.3%	.292
2021 DC	TEX	MLB	27	2	2	20	59	0	61.7	46	8	6.1	12.7	86	34.3%	.292

Comparables: Reyes Moronta, Edwin Díaz, Corey Knebel

Going into the season, there was some question whether Leclerc would remain the team's closer after a rocky 2019. Afterwards, there was no question. He saved one game in his usual shotgun-pellet fashion, and then felt shoulder discomfort warming up for save two, which never came. Rafael Montero seized the role in Texas, so there was little left for the sporadically great Leclerc to do except heal, demonstrate value, and wait for another opportunity. With Montero shipped to Seattle, it may be here already.

YEAR	TEAM	LVL	AGE	WHIP	ERA	DRA-	WARP	MPH	FB%	WHF	CSP
2018	TEX	MLB	24	0.85	1.56	64	1.4	97.4	47.7%	41.1%	
2019	TEX	MLB	25	1.33	4.33	61	1.8	98.5	50.2%	33.0%	
2020	TEX	MLB	26	2.00	4.50	99	0.0	95.9	57.4%	43.8%	
2021 FS	TEX	MLB	27	1.43	4.08	92	0.5	98.1	49.8%	35.5%	43.4%
2021 DC	TEX	MLB	27	1.43	4.08	92	0.6	98.1	49.8%	35.5%	43.4%

Juan Nicasio RHP
Born: 08/31/86   Age: 34   Bats: R   Throws: R
Height: 6'4"   Weight: 250   Origin: International Free Agent, 2006

YEAR	TEAM	LVL	AGE	W	L	SV	G	GS	IP	H	HR	BB/9	K/9	K	GB%	BABIP
2018	SEA	MLB	31	1	6	1	46	0	42	53	6	1.1	11.4	53	35.8%	.402
2019	PHI	MLB	32	2	3	1	47	0	47¹	57	4	4.0	8.6	45	45.6%	.368
2020	TEX	MLB	33	0	0	0	2	0	1¹	5	1	13.5	6.8	1	25.0%	.571
2021 FS	TEX	MLB	34	2	2	0	57	0	50	46	6	2.8	8.2	45	42.0%	.290

Comparables: Tommy Hunter, Wade Davis, Daniel Hudson

It was a brief season for Nicasio even by 2020 standards; it took two weeks for the Rangers to call him up from their alternate site, and two days for him to take personal leave to be with his family in the Dominican Republic. That gave him just long enough to leave a mark, even if it wasn't technically his mark: Nicasio's final batter faced was Fernando Tatis, Jr., who hit a rather newsworthy 3-0 grand slam and sparked the 2,432,935th debate on unwritten rules in baseball.

Texas Rangers 2021

YEAR	TEAM	LVL	AGE	WHIP	ERA	DRA-	WARP	MPH	FB%	WHF	CSP
2018	SEA	MLB	31	1.38	6.00	60	1.1	96.0	70.7%	23.5%	
2019	PHI	MLB	32	1.65	4.75	110	0.0	95.9	54.5%	21.1%	
2020	TEX	MLB	33	5.25	40.50	119	0.0	95.5	67.4%	17.6%	
2021 FS	TEX	MLB	34	1.25	3.71	88	0.6	95.9	60.0%	21.7%	48.9%

Joe Palumbo   LHP

Born: 10/26/94   Age: 26   Bats: L   Throws: L
Height: 6'0"   Weight: 195   Origin: Round 30, 2013 Draft (#910 overall)

YEAR	TEAM	LVL	AGE	W	L	SV	G	GS	IP	H	HR	BB/9	K/9	K	GB%	BABIP
2018	RAN	ROK	23	0	0	0	3	3	9	5	1	1.0	15.0	15	56.2%	.267
2018	DE	HI-A	23	1	4	0	6	6	27	24	3	2.0	11.3	34	41.7%	.304
2018	FRI	AA	23	1	0	0	2	2	9^1	6	0	2.9	9.6	10	39.1%	.261
2019	FRI	AA	24	0	0	0	11	10	53^2	43	5	4.2	11.6	69	39.1%	.311
2019	NAS	AAA	24	3	0	0	6	6	27	13	4	3.3	13.0	39	40.4%	.188
2019	TEX	MLB	24	0	3	0	7	4	16^2	21	7	4.3	11.3	21	34.0%	.333
2020	TEX	MLB	25	0	1	0	2	0	2^1	3	1	11.6	19.3	5	33.3%	.400
2021 FS	TEX	MLB	26	9	8	0	26	26	150	134	23	3.8	10.8	179	38.0%	.304
2021 DC	TEX	MLB	26	1	1	0	9	3	14.7	13	2	3.8	10.8	17	38.0%	.304

Comparables: Thomas Pannone, Yacksel Ríos, Jarlin García

After transferring following his sophomore year in high school, Palumbo had to reclassify as a sophomore thanks to obscure age limitations established by his new private school in West Islip, New York. The reclassification cost him a year of eligibility, making his junior season his final one. In order to get reps as an 18-year-old, Palumbo joined the Long Island Black Sox, a local men's league team, where he was discovered by a Rangers area scout. He was drafted in the 30th round in 2013, and from there he undertook the usual development process. Well, aside from the Tommy John surgery in 2018 and the bouts with ulcerative colitis in 2020. Other than that, Palumbo is just your regular, run-of-the-mill lefty with huge fastball spin and a solid three-pitch mix. Wait, did that say run-of-the-mill? It meant to read "potential mid-rotation starter."

YEAR	TEAM	LVL	AGE	WHIP	ERA	DRA-	WARP	MPH	FB%	WHF	CSP
2018	RAN	ROK	23	0.67	4.00						
2018	DE	HI-A	23	1.11	2.67	63	0.7				
2018	FRI	AA	23	0.96	1.93	74	0.2				
2019	FRI	AA	24	1.27	3.19	74	0.9				
2019	NAS	AAA	24	0.85	2.67	36	1.3				
2019	TEX	MLB	24	1.74	9.18	116	0.0	95.5	56.7%	22.8%	
2020	TEX	MLB	25	2.57	11.57	86	0.0	94.1	57.6%	42.9%	
2021 FS	TEX	MLB	26	1.32	4.05	94	1.9	95.2	56.9%	27.0%	49.1%
2021 DC	TEX	MLB	26	1.32	4.05	94	0.2	95.2	56.9%	27.0%	49.1%

Tyler Phillips   RHP
Born: 10/27/97   Age: 23   Bats: R   Throws: R
Height: 6'5"   Weight: 225   Origin: Round 16, 2015 Draft (#468 overall)

YEAR	TEAM	LVL	AGE	W	L	SV	G	GS	IP	H	HR	BB/9	K/9	K	GB%	BABIP
2018	HIC	LO-A	20	11	5	0	22	22	128	117	4	1.0	8.7	124	52.8%	.308
2019	DE	HI-A	21	2	2	0	6	6	37^2	28	1	1.4	6.7	28	54.3%	.262
2019	FRI	AA	21	7	9	0	18	16	93^1	95	15	1.9	7.1	74	50.9%	.292
2021 FS	*TEX*	*MLB*	*23*	*2*	*2*	*0*	*57*	*0*	*50*	*49*	*7*	*2.5*	*6.9*	*38*	*46.3%*	*.284*
2021 DC	*TEX*	*MLB*	*23*	*3*	*2*	*0*	*30*	*3*	*26.7*	*26*	*4*	*2.5*	*6.9*	*20*	*46.3%*	*.284*

Comparables: Rony García, Gabriel Ynoa, Joe Ross

The Rangers protected Phillips from the Rule 5 draft heading into 2020, despite the righty struggling in his first taste of advanced competition at Double-A. His pitch mix says starter, and his stats say he has good control, but his command within the zone might not be able to protect him from a role in middle relief.

YEAR	TEAM	LVL	AGE	WHIP	ERA	DRA-	WARP	MPH	FB%	WHF	CSP
2018	HIC	LO-A	20	1.02	2.67	64	3.2				
2019	DE	HI-A	21	0.90	1.19	71	0.7				
2019	FRI	AA	21	1.23	4.72	108	-0.4				
2021 FS	*TEX*	*MLB*	*23*	*1.27*	*3.91*	*95*	*0.4*				
2021 DC	*TEX*	*MLB*	*23*	*1.27*	*3.91*	*95*	*0.3*				

Texas Rangers 2021

Cole Winn RHP
Born: 11/25/99 Age: 21 Bats: R Throws: R
Height: 6'2" Weight: 190 Origin: Round 1, 2018 Draft (#15 overall)

YEAR	TEAM	LVL	AGE	W	L	SV	G	GS	IP	H	HR	BB/9	K/9	K	GB%	BABIP
2019	HIC	LO-A	19	4	4	0	18	18	68^2	59	5	5.1	8.5	65	46.6%	.292
2021 FS	TEX	MLB	21	2	3	0	57	0	50	48	8	6.7	7.5	41	41.9%	.280

Comparables: Max Fried, Tyler Chatwood, Luke Jackson

It must be strange dominating as a prep arm, chucking mid-90s heat with excellent command, being selected in the first round of the MLB Draft and not even be the most successful right-handed pitcher from your own high school. Such is the case for Winn, who donned the same red, gold, and white of the Lutheran Lancers in Orange County as Gerrit Cole. He did show improvement over the course of his first season as a pro, posting a 2.56 ERA while nearly striking out a batter per inning in his last seven starts of 2019. Of course, it's difficult to gauge how any young hurler will handle a season spent in noncompetitive action at his team's alternate site, but less wear and tear on a young arm is probably not a bad thing, and if the extra development and coaching could help Winn trim a few free passes from his walk rate, he could remain on track to fulfill his destiny as a mid-to-backend starter in Arlington sometime soon.

YEAR	TEAM	LVL	AGE	WHIP	ERA	DRA-	WARP	MPH	FB%	WHF	CSP
2019	HIC	LO-A	19	1.43	4.46	112	-0.2				
2021 FS	TEX	MLB	21	1.71	5.72	127	-0.5				

Rangers Prospects

The State of the System:
We tend to like the Rangers' system more than most. But it's maybe not quite as fun/deep as recent vintages.

The Top Ten:

1 ── ★ ★ ★ *2021 Top 101 Prospect* **#26** ★ ★ ★ ──
Leody Taveras CF OFP: 60 ETA: Debuted in 2020
Born: 09/08/98 Age: 22 Bats: S Throws: R Height: 6'2" Weight: 195
Origin: International Free Agent, 2015

The Report: Taveras has long tantalized, flashing all five-tools as a switch-hitting center fielder while never really imposing his will on opposing pitchers at any minor league stop. The defensive tools did more than flash and we were always confident he would at least be a plus center fielder given his high-end plus speed and above-average throwing arm. Taveras would flash plus raw power from both sides, but never slugged over .400 at any level. He was never overmatched at the plate and improved his approach and quality of contact as he moved up levels, always young for his league. Age-relative-to-league only gets you so far—as does noting that Down East is a terrible place to hit and his line there in 2019 was 24 percent better than league average by DRC+—and there were those on staff who saw Taveras and thought he would just be a glove-first, average regular in center field.

Development Track: Well Taveras still hasn't slugged .400 at any level, but he posted a career high .395—with a .168 ISO—after getting handed the everyday center field gig in September for the Rangers. It was the hit tool that actually let him down a bit, as the K-rate ballooned seeing major league offspeed for the first time. It was a big jump for the bat, and there's some positives to take away there going forward. The glove was as-advertised as Taveras immediately looked like a Gold Glove candidate in center field. There isn't as much clarity here as you'd like, and Taveras remains a bit of a Rorsrach test, you can still see the potential All-Star, or the Role-5 glove guy if you stare at his 2020 season.

Variance: Low. Taveras didn't really answer the questions about his bat in the majors, but the glove and speed will keep him manning center in Texas for a while, and he flashed some more of the raw power in games while not being completely overmatched in what was a pretty big jump in difficulty.

Mark Barry's Fantasy Take: Taveras might still be better IRL than in fantasy, but two notable takeaways from his first bout against big-league pitching could portend to future fantasy success: 1) He played great defense in center field, which automatically extends his audition, and 2) He stole eight bases in 33 games without being caught. If he can figure out how to scale back on the strikeouts, the steals alone give him OF3 upside.

─────── ★ ★ ★ *2021 Top 101 Prospect* **#56** ★ ★ ★ ───────

2
Josh Jung   3B   OFP: 60   ETA: 2021, service time manipulation TBD
Born: 02/12/98   Age: 23   Bats: R   Throws: R   Height: 6'2"   Weight: 215
Origin: Round 1, 2019 Draft (#8 overall)

The Report: You know those posts you keep seeing during these pandemic times from that one really annoying friend about "If you didn't grind you wasted time" or some variant? Jung must have seen one and taken that to heart. Coming into the year, Jung's major concerns were whether he'd hit for enough power to be a top-level corner infield prospect. Working at Texas' alternate site, Jung answered that with a yes. Without major swing changes, Jung began driving the ball more to all fields. There was minimal doubt about his ability to make contact, but the development of real above-average power is a huge add to his toolbox.

Defensively, nothing has changed much. Jung played both shortstop and third base at Texas Tech before moving exclusively to the hot corner post draft. Jung has the range and quickness to handle the position without being anywhere near a liability. Is there some room for improvement? Most likely, but that upward movement would take him from above league average to potential Gold Glove. Whether that is feasible seems difficult to foresee, but with the improvements at the plate the current defensive level is more than palatable.

Development Track: If Jung's power was the $64,000 question, this is the $32,000. Texas has finally said what everyone watching already knew: The rebuild is on. This includes the moving of Gold Glove winner Isiah Kiner-Falefa from third base to shortstop replacing veteran Elvis Andrus. That leaves a large, No. 2-prospect-shaped-hole at the hot corner. Jung is ready to take that spot, Texas is ready for him to do it, but nothing is official yet.

Variance: Medium. Low doesn't feel right post pandemic 2020, but folks who saw Jung pre-2020 saw the potential of what appears to have happened. So, split the difference.

Mark Barry's Fantasy Take: This guy has grown on me. I'm not sure why I came in so "meh" on Jung, but every time I come back to his player card and read reports, I like him a little more each time. I think right now is the last time you'll be able to scoop him up at anything resembling fair market value, and I'd even be willing to pay a slight premium, especially with rumblings that Jung has found a bit of pop.

★ ★ ★ *2021 Top 101 Prospect* **#60** ★ ★ ★

3 **Dane Dunning** **RHP** OFP: 60 ETA: Debuted in 2020
Born: 12/20/94 Age: 26 Bats: R Throws: R Height: 6'4" Weight: 225
Origin: Round 1, 2016 Draft (#29 overall)

The Report: Before his Tommy John surgery in March 2019, Dunning was knocking on the door of the majors with a solid four-pitch mix headlined by a sinker he could move effectively around the zone and a potential plus changeup. He was a typical mid-rotation starter prospect with a durable frame and better command and change than that profile typically features in Double-A. Conversely Dunning was maybe a little short on the fastball velocity and breaking ball projection. The uncertainty of the surgery knocked him off our national list coming into the season, but there was little reason to believe he wouldn't be an above-average major league starter assuming a normal rehab.

Development Track: Dunning's rehab went well enough that he was moved into the major league rotation down the stretch and made seven, well, above-average starts for the White Sox. He moved his low-90s fastball around the zone well enough, and improvements in both the slider and curve gave him two potential average-or-better breaking ball looks. The change still flashed plus although it was used relatively sparingly in the majors. Dunning should slot right into the 2021 Rangers rotation when he will be two years removed from the surgery. We'll know a lot more by this time next year, but the mid-rotation projection still looks good for now.

Variance: Medium. The command, secondary feel and overall stamina aren't quite all the way back coming off surgery, but we're fairly confident Dunning is at least an average major league starter.

Mark Barry's Fantasy Take: Dunning was one of the biggest surprises and best stories of the 2020 season, for my money, though he doesn't figure to be more than an SP4/5. He struck out over a batter per inning this past season and had a solid swinging-strike rate at 11.4 percent, but he doesn't get many swings outside the strike zone and has middling control numbers. Dunning posted a 4.25 DRA, which speaks to his run-of-the-mill fantasy profile. However, it doesn't seem that fantasy analysts are getting too excited about the right-hander. He sits outside the Top 250 in redraft leagues and outside the Top 400 in dynasty rankings. That seems about right, as it's hard to see too much upside unless his changeup takes a significant step forward.

★ ★ ★ *2021 Top 101 Prospect* **#98** ★ ★ ★

4 **Sam Huff** **C** OFP: 60 ETA: Debuted in 2020
Born: 01/14/98 Age: 23 Bats: R Throws: R Height: 6'5" Weight: 240
Origin: Round 7, 2016 Draft (#219 overall)

The Report: In his short stint in the majors following a surprising September call-up, Huff did exactly what he did in the minors: He showed strong power, struck out a decent amount, and didn't walk, while displaying average catcher defense with the potential for more down the road. That's the Huff profile in a nutshell. Off the field is where the work was stacked for the young backstop. The Rangers noted that Huff—and all catchers at the alternate site—were working with coaches daily putting together game plans for the pitching matchups across the street. The goal was to accelerate the mental side of the position, cutting down the learning curve for baseball's most difficult position. There's a good chance the biggest growth in Texas' potential future catcher is something unseen, but something necessary all the same.

Development Track: Huff's growth was described as "steady," which is good. That also means, based on where Huff was pre-pandemic, that major league readiness is still a ways off. Huff needs to be facing age- and level-appropriate competition in real games, something that the alternate site could only simulate. If Huff can go to Double A as the starting catcher in 2021, we'll learn a lot more. There's a chance, albeit a small one, that Huff could be given the backup job behind Jose Trevino in Arlington. That seems less than ideal, barring an extreme playing time split. Huff needs to play every day somewhere, preferably somewhere more representative of his current skills.

Variance: High. Huff's chance of moving off catcher feel less likely than before, but that still means he's going to have to make improvements to be a plus regular. That means fewer strikeouts, higher quality of contact, and continued growth behind the plate. That's a lot to ask of any player, and the various ways the profile could go sideways dictate a high variance designation.

Mark Barry's Fantasy Take: If Huff can maintain the .355/.394/.742 line that he posted upon his debut, he'll have a very bright future as a fantasy catcher. He still struck out a ton, though, so it's more likely that he'll come back to earth and hover in that range of other decent fantasy backstops, spending some seasons in the top 5-10 at the position and others as a streamer, easily replaceable with someone fresh from the wire.

5. Cole Winn   RHP   OFP: 60   ETA: 2022
Born: 11/25/99   Age: 21   Bats: R   Throws: R   Height: 6'2"   Weight: 190
Origin: Round 1, 2018 Draft (#15 overall)

The Report: Winn is a four pitch starting pitching prospect with his fastball checking in as the best pitch in his arsenal along with a changeup, slider, and curveball. He's had an uneven development curve since being drafted, but If Jung had the best alternate site performance, Winn was right alongside him. His ascent this year came for a few reasons. One of the big factors is time: Winn just turned 21 this past November, and more time in the organization has aided his development. Winn better understands what he is and isn't.

Which leads to one of his major improvements: throwing more strikes. Winn previously held a mentality of avoiding contact entirely, and as a result would throw more pitches outside the zone than necessary. Hitters caught up to that some, and as a result would put him in awkward situations that forced him to throw less-than-ideal pitches in the zone. This year, Winn spent time learning how to be more cerebral with his pitch mix along with utilizing his whole arsenal to get more weak contact on those in zone pitches.

Development Track: Winn hasn't pitched above Low-A yet, which matters for a Texas organization that over the last two years has decelerated its upward pitcher movement through the minors. Even a strong alternate site showing probably means Winn is heading to either High-A or Double-A to start 2021, and is likely to spend his entire season below the bigs. That said, his 2020 progress is enough that barring more issues it's not impossible to dream on a 2022 debut for Winn.

Variance: High. So much of this year's results are hard to put in the frame, but Winn's growth is encouraging. He's not risk proof, because no pitcher is. That said, this is probably the best to feel about Winn since he got drafted.

Mark Barry's Fantasy Take: It would be nice if Winn's proclivity to throw more strikes translated into real games, but I don't know if that will necessarily help his fantasy profile. Seems like a pretty clear back-end starter for me.

6. Justin Foscue 2B   OFP: 55   ETA: Late 2022 / Early 2023
Born: 03/02/99   Age: 22   Bats: R   Throws: R   Height: 6'0"   Weight: 203
Origin: Round 1, 2020 Draft (#14 overall)

The Report: As one of the best second basemen in all of college baseball in 2019, it still felt weird to hear Foscue's name called so early in the first round by the Rangers. In a year where certainty was hard to find in the draft, taking a big time producer from the SEC at a position with a low bar for expectations became a valuable commodity for the Rangers. Foscue can probably play some third base or shortstop in a pinch, but the hitting potential might up his value considering the pull power he can get to is seldom found in most of today's second sackers.

Development Track: Another selling point on his draft card has to be the juxtaposition of his baseball maturity (advanced) against his relative youth as a young-for-his-class junior. The latter likely helped buoy his draft stock for algorithmically-inclined teams, which is to say perhaps he has more at the end of his rope while still being ahead of the curve.

Variance: Low. Could he put together an All-Star campaign? Sure, why not. What he offers is a high floor with a modest ceiling, and every team trying to compete needs these guys somewhere on the roster.

Mark Barry's Fantasy Take: Best case scenario, Foscue gives you something like a Cesar Hernandez-y line. Worst case scenario, how do you feel about the Bryson Stott experience in Philadelphia? There might be hits, but there might not be much else.

7 Anderson Tejeda   SS   OFP: 55   ETA: Debuted in 2020
Born: 05/01/98   Age: 23   Bats: S   Throws: R   Height: 6'0"   Weight: 200
Origin: International Free Agent, 2014

The Report: What a difference a year makes. Last year, Tejeda was outside the top 10 in part because of a shoulder injury. Now, he's put a major-league debut in his rear view mirror before playing a minor league game above High-A. Tejeda shares a lot of qualities at the plate with Huff: He strikes out a lot, doesn't walk a lot, but can hit the snot out of the ball when he squares it up. The difference for Tejeda is his defense is more advanced. Tejeda is capable of handling second base, shortstop, and probably even third base if given the opportunity. He's an electric defender who uses quickness, athleticism, and a hard to quantify fearlessness to cover anywhere on the infield. The question for Tejeda will be if he can hit for enough power across a full season to cover the approach and contact deficiencies. But if Tejeda is going to be a long term starter and not just a fifth infield type, who can play all over the diamond when called upon, his plate discipline will need to improve.

Development Track: Tejeda's 2020 debut signaled the start of Texas going young. Tejeda now has every opportunity to find his way onto the major league roster full time in 2021. The exact role is cloudy though.

Variance: Medium. The offensive issues for Tejeda are well known, and he's either going to fix them or not. That said, those problems will determine starter versus bench and that's not an insignificant gap.

Mark Barry's Fantasy Take: If Tejeda gets his swing-and-miss under control, he's a sneaky-good power/speed option at MI. If not, I guess he's still a sneaky power/speed option, but not necessarily a good one. Maybe, like, Niko Goodrum with fewer walks? Does that tickle your fancy?

8 Evan Carter   OFP: 55   ETA: 2024
Born: 08/29/02   Age: 18   Bats: L   Throws: R   Height: 6'4"   Weight: 190
Origin: Round 2, 2020 Draft (#50 overall)

The Report: Our focus on the Baseball Prospectus Prospect Team is pro coverage, but we usually at least know of almost everyone picked during Day 1 of the draft. The Rangers' selection of Evan Carter at 50 elicited "who?" from much more embedded amateur evaluators than us. We did manage to source a third-hand report, and while there is always risk in that kind of game of telephone, Carter appeared to be a steal in the second round with a potential plus hit tool driving the profile.

Development Track: No one remains an unknown for long in the prospect world, and Carter crushed the instructional league, standing shoulder to shoulder with other first-round picks with the bat. This ranking feels super aggressive, but I suspect it will look overly conservative by June of 2021.

Variance: Extreme. Carter didn't play like a virtually unknown second rounder at instructs, but even if the Rangers snagged an extra first round talent with the bat, that first round talent is still a prep that hasn't played in a real professional game yet.

Mark Barry's Fantasy Take: Your guess is as good as mine about how Carter's status will be viewed in the dynasty world. At the very least he seems like a great breakout candidate who you should absolutely be ready to pounce on early in the 2021 season.

9 Kyle Cody RHP OFP: 55 ETA: Debuted in 2020
Born: 08/09/94 Age: 26 Bats: R Throws: R Height: 6'7" Weight: 225
Origin: Round 6, 2016 Draft (#189 overall)

The Report: Cody was one of our favorite prospects based on 2017 live looks. At the time, he was throwing a bowling ball sinker that got up into the mid-90s, and both his breaking ball and changeup were flashing at least above-average. Tommy John surgery in 2018 wiped out most of his next two seasons, and it was honestly a bit of a surprise when the Rangers added him to the 40-man last offseason given that he was 25 with no experience above A-ball and coming off two lost seasons.

Development Track: He popped up in the majors down the stretch, initially in the bullpen and then stretched out for starts as long as five innings. While his extremely shiny ERA was mostly a mirage, he still posted an above-average DRA. The stuff was largely as I remembered—fastball up to the mid-90s with sink and a flashing breaking ball and change, though the former is more slidery now. He's not going to be a whiff machine and the command needs to tighten, but Cody just might be a decent MLB starting pitcher already.

Variance: Medium. He pretty much is what he is, except for latent durability concerns.

Mark Barry's Fantasy Take: The excitement ends here. Cody is a cool story, but I'm not sure you have to worry about him in a fantasy sense.

10 Tyler Phillips RHP OFP: 55 ETA: 2022
Born: 10/27/97 Age: 23 Bats: R Throws: R Height: 6'5" Weight: 225
Origin: Round 16, 2015 Draft (#468 overall)

The Report: Coming into 2020, Phillips was a command first pitcher with good, not great stuff who tended to get knocked around every time the command wobbled. The offseason and alternate site time was dedicated to figuring out why that was. The fastball was a prime offender; Phillips throws a four seam, but the velocity and spin rate made it look like a two-seam. This season, Phillips focused on adding more carry and spin to the pitch. That resulted in more vertical movement, making it harder to hit. This also happened with Phillips' curveball, which was flat at times last year making it a less desirable offering. To pair with all this verticality, Phillips is now throwing a slider as well. The mixture of horizontal and vertical made a big difference for Phillips, who paired this with his already mature approach to show great strides over his inconsistent 2019.

Development Track: Phillips made all these changes, but until he can road test them against real opposition it'll be hard to say more about how effective they are. Phillips probably took a step forward this season, but 2021 will be the proof in the pudding.

Variance: Low. Phillips had a high floor already, and was likely to see a fifth starter-type role even before the changes he made this year. The improvements this year could see an improvement to that projection, but it's more marginal than most.

Mark Barry's Fantasy Take: Another right-handed, potential back-end starter? Sure, why not?

The Prospects You Meet Outside The Top Ten

Top Ten Prospects in a shallower (or literally the White Sox) system

Sherten Apostel   3B   Born: 03/11/99   Age: 22   Bats: R   Throws: R   Height: 6'4"   Weight: 235   Origin: International Free Agent, 2018
Another who got a look in the big leagues this year, Apostel still hits the ball hard and still shows a surprisingly strong aptitude for defense. Between trades and internal growth, the system grew in strength which forced Apostel down the list some. He'd still be a Top Ten player in most systems, which says more about how Texas improved on the farm this year.

Avery Weems   LHP   Born: 06/06/97   Age: 24   Bats: R   Throws: L   Height: 6'2"   Weight: 205   Origin: Round 6, 2019 Draft (#170 overall)
The other piece in the Lance Lynn deal, Weems got squeezed out from a spot at the White Sox alternate site but looked unhittable in instructs, showing a bit more velocity than he had in college. He'l be ticketed for full-season ball in 2021 and could be a fast mover if the Rangers choose to make him a full-time reliever immediately. He offers 95 from the left side and an absolutely wipeout breaker.

Prospects to dream on a little

Ricky Vanasco   RHP   Born: 10/13/98   Age: 22   Bats: R   Throws: R   Height: 6'3"   Weight: 180   Origin: Round 15, 2017 Draft (#464 overall)

Vanasco was on his way to a Top Ten spot on the list this season, after an impressive showing at the alternate site. Then in September, Vanasco had Tommy John surgery, which means we won't see if what he did at the alternate site will translate into games until 2022.

Keithron Moss   2B   Born: 08/20/01   Age: 19   Bats: S   Throws: R   Height: 5'11"   Weight: 165   Origin: International Free Agent, 2017

A Baby Ranger with a lot of hype, Moss continues to be one to watch. His speed is the lead, but improved defense and contact are helping fill out the profile. The second base/shortstop combo is one of many infielder-with-upside types who populate the lowest levels of the system.

Jonathan Ornelas   3B   Born: 05/26/00   Age: 21   Bats: R   Throws: R   Height: 6'1"   Weight: 178   Origin: Round 3, 2018 Draft (#91 overall)

The 21-year-old infielder also has a lot of buzz right now. Ornelas faded down the stretch in 2019, a season in which he got the most playing time of his career. As he matures, his body is filling out particularly in his upper half. In a system overloaded with potential standout infielders, Ornelas is one of the most intriguing prospects in that group and like many of them, can handle himself at three different spots on the dirt.

Ronny Henriquez   RHP   Born: 06/20/00   Age: 21   Bats: R   Throws: R   Height: 5'10"   Weight: 155   Origin: International Free Agent, 2017

A diminutive dealer, Henriquez is a fastball first pitcher who attacks hitters. Over the last year, Henriquez improved on his changeup while working at the Texas spring training complex. The 20-year-old will need more seasoning, with only 19 starts above the Dominican Summer League. Henriquez does have a high ceiling, low floor profile that could provide an exciting reliever if starting doesn't work out.

MLB arms, but probably relievers

Hans Crouse   RHP   Born: 09/15/98   Age: 22   Bats: L   Throws: R   Height: 6'4"   Weight: 180   Origin: Round 2, 2017 Draft (#66 overall)

A lot of factors played into Crouse going from Top Ten stalwart to others receiving vote(s). One was Crouse missed some time near the end of a season that was already going to have limited developmental opportunities. Another is that his home is looking more likely to be the bullpen. Crouse has a military grade arm, but as he continues his journey, it appears that his future could likely resemble that of current reliever Jonathan Hernandez. If that was the case, Texas should still be pleased.

Owen White   RHP   Born: 08/09/99   Age: 21   Bats: R   Throws: R   Height: 6'3"   Weight: 170   Origin: Round 2, 2018 Draft (#55 overall)

The former second-round pick had Tommy John surgery in 2019, so his future is quite nebulous. That said, White appears ready to go for whatever 2021 will look like. When he does, White will bring a good fastball and slider to the mix. He could be destined for Low-A Down East; that was his likely first stop pre-surgery.

The Bonus Babies

Maximo Acosta   SS   Born: 10/29/02   Age: 18   Bats: R   Throws: R   Height: 6'1"   Weight: 170   Origin: International Free Agent, 2019

One of a pair of mysteriously intriguing prospects in Texas' system along, Acosta got some field time stateside at the most recent instructional league in Arizona. The 18-year-old looked like a teenager with minimal pro experience. The defense showed positive signs; Acosta is a plus athlete who will build on that profile with age and body maturation. The bat still has a way to go as well, with the more fine skills like pitch recognition still in development.

Bayron Lora   RF   Born: 09/29/02   Age: 18   Bats: R   Throws: R   Height: 6'3"   Weight: 190   Origin: International Free Agent, 2019

Lora, meanwhile, had a less-than-favorable appearance in Arizona. The bat looked overmatched and lacked the power expected form a 6-foot-5 outfielder. The defensive profile is still a mystery, as is much of what Lora brings to the table. That's not necessarily a warning bell, but more of a caution sign. Young players need time, and in the case of Lora it's best to be patient and watch.

Top Talents 25 and Under (as of 4/1/2021):

1. Leody Taveras, OF
2. Josh Jung, 3B
3. Dane Dunning, RHP
4. Sam Huff, C
5. Cole Winn, RHP
6. Nate Lowe, 1B
7. Justin Foscue, IF
8. Anderson Tejeda, SS
9. Evan Carter, OF
10. Kyle Cody, RHP

Had the Rangers not traded for Nate Lowe, it's possible that they wouldn't have had any non-rookie make this list. With Kolby Allard bombing out as a starter, Jonathan Hernandez would've been the best candidate, and he's a reliever, even if he looks like he might be turning into a good one.

But they did trade for Lowe, and he's pretty clearly worthy ranking somewhere on the 25U. The Rays never gave him a clean opportunity at a full-time job, and he hasn't been stellar in the majors in limited chances. He's a three true outcomes slugger and likely to be a useful power bat for at least the rest of his 20s.

Part 3: Featured Articles

Rangers All-Time Top 10 Players

by Steven Goldman

POSITION PLAYERS

JIM SUNDBERG, C (1974-1983, 1988-1989)

Sundberg was a durable catcher who routinely caught 140 or 150 games a year. He was in the lineup more for his glove than his bat, but he wasn't an automatic out either; unfortunately, we can never know how he might have hit had he been given an occasional day off. He won six Gold Gloves with the Rangers and when he retired was third on the career list for games caught behind his contemporaries Bob Boone and Carlton Fisk.

IVAN RODRIGUEZ, C (1991-2002, 2009)

The all-time leader in games and hits as a catcher, his glove got him to the majors as a teenager and his bat trailed along after. He hit only .266/.301/.379 in his first three seasons, but in 1994 he began an offensive expansion of his capabilities that was almost linear, his productivity outpacing a rapidly-inflating league context. From then through 2004 he hit .315/.357/.513 in over 1,400 games with batting averages between .297 and (in an injury-shortened 2000) .347. Subsequently the sheer weight of games caught began to tell on him and since he never evolved much in the way of patience, his bat couldn't support the decline of his batting average. The memory of his defensive skills kept him playing anyway. As we wrote in 2012, "We at BP salute anyone who can put on the pads and catch one game in Arlington in August, much less 140 games a year for the better part of two decades."

RAFAEL PALMEIRO, 1B (1989-1993, 1999-2003)

He was a great story for a while, a former first-round pick who hit .307 in his first full season in the majors but was dismissed by the Cubs because of his lack of power. Thus are negative incentives inflicted upon the mind, but that understanding awaited subsequent revelations. Until then, it seemed as if Palmeiro had had the last laugh. He hit .290/.378/.519 in two stints with the Rangers and, bizarrely, won a Gold Glove in 1999 despite getting only 28 games in the field. He had over 3,000 hits to go with his 10 seasons of hitting from 37 to 47 home runs (only Babe Ruth and Henry Aaron had more) and surely PEDs were not responsible for all of that, but it was his own finger-wagging insistence denial to Congress in 2005 that made it difficult to put it all in perspective. Cheating in this context is an amorphous concept; hypocrisy is not.

IAN KINSLER, 2B (2006-2013)

A draft afterthought tabbed in 2003's 17th round, Kinsler shocked everyone, including perhaps himself, with his hitting prowess—a 60-game stretch averaging .402 will open eyes, even if it comes in the Midwest League. He was just as surprising in the majors, sometimes sacrificing contact for power and hitting as many as 32 home runs, sometimes emphasizing contact and hitting .319 with doubles power. His defense, however, was consistent in its excellence. He scored over 100 runs six times, won two Gold Gloves, and his Rangers teams were some of the most successful in team history. He has a decent argument for a Hall of Fame berth.

BUDDY BELL, 3B (1979-1985, 1989)

Vastly underrated, Bell came up with Cleveland during their purgatorial years and was traded to the Rangers for fellow third baseman Toby Harrah. The latter was a good player, but he wasn't as good as Bell, a defensive standout who won the Gold Glove in all six of his full seasons in Arlington. He hit too, .293/.351/.431 as a Ranger, about 20 percent above league average when era and environment are accounted for. He was a contact hitter who filled out good batting averages with doubles and a dozen or so home runs per year, a type presently absent from the game and much missed.

ADRIAN BELTRE, 3B (2011-2018)

He came up so young that his career had several distinct phases; it's easy to forget that he played more games for the Rangers than he did for any other team. Signing him was something of a gamble. His years in Seattle had been disappointing and his comeback season in Boston, while excellent, might have proved to be a one-off. Moreover, signing a 32-year-old to a five-year contract is often a sucker's bet. It was one the Rangers won; Beltre aged slowly and gracefully, hitting .304/.357/.509 and retaining his defensive excellence over a stay that was extended to eight years. A popular presence both for the fans in the stands and the players in the dugout, Beltre was one of the few players who left on his own terms rather than overstaying his welcome, surpassing 3,000 hits but leaving 500 home runs and the all-time record for games played at third base on the table rather than letting us see him stagger, Biggio-like, to the finish.

TOBY HARRAH, SS/3B (1969, 1971-1978, 1985-1986)
Drafted off the Phillies' roster and rushed to the majors before he was ready, Harrah did his growing up in public. Going on 25, he had hit .250/.316/.327 in 369 games. It was a low-offense era, so the results weren't quite as bad as they look today, but they were far from good. Things began to click into place in 1974, and from there through 1982 Harrah proved capable of a valuable combination of power, speed, and patience, hitting .272/.375/.424. The power came and went and so did the stolen-base percentages, but 80-plus walks a year were a constant. He and Bell were traded for each other in December 1978. Over the next five years, Harrah hit .281/.383/.417 for Cleveland, Bell .298/.353/.442 for Texas. It's almost a wash, except that Bell was a great defender while fielding was always the weakest part of Harrah's game, so the Rangers won the challenge trade 29.1 WARP to 17.5.

ELVIS ANDRUS, SS (2009-2020)
Departs the Rangers as second all-time on the franchise list of games played. A good all-around shortstop who seemingly peaked as a slightly above-average offensive player in 2016-2017 (he hit .299/.348/.457 in 305 games), the team's decision to sign him to an eight-year, $120 million contract in April 2013 was odd, a risky bet that he'd continue to maintain his defensive skills and undergo an unlikely offensive expansion—what he eventually gave them in the latter regard was fleeting and strictly in the good-not-great lane. They didn't lose the gamble, but they didn't win it either. We can be less equivocal about various managers giving him over 1000 starts batting first, second, or third in the order.

FRANK HOWARD, OF/1B (1965-1972)
A bespectacled 6-foot-7 behemoth with extraordinary power, Hondo was miscast in the low-offense late 1960s and early 1970s. He'd have been better suited to our time when he could have hit balls over buildings without much effort. A free swinger by the standards of his day, he was traded from the Dodgers to the Washington Senators as something of a disappointment—powerful, but one-dimensional. Managers Gil Hodges, Jim Lemon, and Ted Williams worked with him in succession; the first two improved his mechanics, the last convinced him to be more selective. Howard, a future coach, was a good student. As the game's offensive levels cratered, Howard was taking off: From 1967 through 1971 he hit .278/.374/.433 (164 OPS+) with 198 home runs. For those four seasons his home-run totals were 36, 44, 48, and 44. He followed the team to Texas in 1972, but at 35 he was beginning to decline and was sold to the playoff-bound Tigers in August.

JUAN GONZALEZ, OF (1989-1999, 2002-2003)
"Juan Gone" was bashing 40-plus homers a year even before the game's offensive levels started to get out of hand in the late 1990s. He hit 434 career home runs, over half of them coming in the five seasons he hit between 42 and

47 of them for the Rangers. A career .295 hitter, he wasn't quite as valuable as his home-run and RBI totals would suggest because he never learned to take a walk and he was a stiff, limited player in the outfield. He won the 1996 and 1998 AL MVP awards, but by WARP he was less than half as valuable as Alex Rodriguez in the former season and was about the same distance behind Albert Belle in the latter.

PITCHERS

FERGUSON JENKINS, RHP (1974-1975, 1978-1981)

He arrived in Arlington from Chicago in a trade that was a win for both sides: The Cubs got third-base prospect Bill Madlock, who won two batting titles for them, and the Rangers got an all-time great pitcher who still had life in his arm despite being subjected to almost insanely heavy workloads. His first season with the Rangers was his best; he led the American League with 25 wins and turned in a 2.82 ERA in 328.1 innings. Swapped back and forth with the Red Sox, he returned to the team at 35 and gave them one more strong season plus a couple more at the league-average innings-eater level.

GAYLORD PERRY, RHP (1975-1977, 1980)

Everyone's favorite Vaseline-baller aged exceedingly well, maintaining a high level of effectiveness into his 40s. His stay was brief because he got caught up in ownership's money woes—the team spent $100,000 to acquire him for Cleveland, then realized it really, really needed the cash and sold him off again for $125,000—but he was nonetheless effective, pitching to a 3.23 ERA in 672.1 innings. Returning at 41 after yet another trade (having received his second Cy Young Award in the interim) he was still effective before being traded to the Yankees in August. He's the team's all-time ERA leader but he's also one of several great pitchers who toiled for the Rangers but did their best work elsewhere.

JON MATLACK, LHP (1978-1983)

The Mets' first-round draft pick in 1967 (the Senators, picking next, took high school catcher Johnny Jones, an Olympic-level failure of scouting; he hit .150 with a single home run in 508 professional plate appearances), Matlack was dealt to the Rangers in a four-way trade that was part of the Mets' late-70s fire-sale. The deal cost the Rangers Bert Blyleven, who had pitched exceedingly well for them but was felt to be unsustainably expensive at the time. In the short term, Matlack made it all seem worthwhile with a 2.27 ERA in 270 innings his first year with the team. The inevitable arm problems ensued and Matlack was able to give the team only one more quality season, though he remained with the club for another five years.

CHARLIE HOUGH, RHP (1980-1990)

Purchased from the Dodgers in July 1980 after a decade spent mostly in the bullpen, the Rangers shifted the 34-year-old knuckleballer to the rotation in 1982 and got a half-dozen seasons of excellence somewhat compromised by their inability to find a catcher who could handle him. The knuckler allowed Hough to be an innings-eater; in 1987 he became the last pitcher to date to start 40 games in a season. He set up the flutterball with a 76-mph fastball. With the sheer abundance of great arms in the game today, we're unlikely to see his like again. More than 30 years after he last pitched for the Rangers, Hough remains the franchise's all-time wins leader with 139.

JOSÉ GUZMÁN, RHP (1985-1992)

The Rangers unveiled many high-profile pitching prospects in the mid-1980s. Guzmán was one of the few to establish himself as a high-level pitcher. Unfortunately, all-too-frequent shoulder problems limited him to just three seasons of 200 innings.

KEVIN BROWN, RHP (1986, 1988-1994)

The Rangers tabbed Brown with the fourth-overall pick of the 1986 draft and scored the bargain of the round (although Gary Sheffield, picked sixth, was close behind). Never wholly appreciated despite a long career that saw him win two ERA titles, Brown was the rare pitcher who could both induce grounders and strikeouts. His rise to dominance was a slow one; although he posted a 3.35 ERA at 24, over the next two seasons his effectiveness diminished as his strikeout-walk ratio trended towards even. Finding a new aggressiveness at 27, he improved his command and emerged as an ace, going 21-11 with a 3.32 ERA in 265.2 innings. He had many more years of greatness in front of them, though most were not with the Rangers after he departed as a free agent following the 1994 season.

NOLAN RYAN, RHP (1989-1993)

Signed as a free agent when he was going on 42, the hope was that Ryan would hang on long enough to pick up his 300th win in a Rangers uniform. He far exceeded that wish, striking out 301 in his first year with the team, reaching the wins milestone in his second, and continuing on for another three seasons, although not even his famously dedicated conditioning regimen and once-in-a-generation arm (maybe once in two or three generations) could keep age at bay indefinitely.

KENNY ROGERS, LHP (1989-1995, 2000-2002, 2004-2005)

A prickly personality who seemed to go out of his way to alienate teammates, managers, and the media alike, Rogers nevertheless made it through 20 years in the major leagues despite these conflicts and bouts of ineffectiveness. He was arguably a better pitcher in his late 30s and early 40s than he was in his 20s. The Rangers largely kept him in the bullpen in those years, but not for lack of trying—when they gave him nine starts in 1991 he was thrashed to the tune of a 7.53 ERA. With the help of pitching coach Claude Osteen he made the jump in 1993 and added an exclamation point on July 28, 1994 when he pitched the first perfect game ever by an AL left-hander. Never overpowering, he mixed his pitches well and became increasingly adept at inducing grounders. He remains the team's all-time leader in games pitched and second in wins and innings pitched.

RICK HELLING, RHP (1994-1996, 1997-2001)
Selected by the Rangers with the 22nd pick of the 1992 draft, Helling dramatically failed three major league auditions from 1994-1996, walking 35 and striking out 46 in 84.2 innings; his ERA was 6.38. They gave up on him at that point, shipping him to the Marlins with Ryan Dempster in return for John Burkett. He showed immediate, albeit short-term improvement, and less than a year later, the Marlins gave up too, stamping him RETURN TO SENDER in exchange for spot lefty Ed Vosberg. Helling was left unprotected in that fall's expansion draft but was not chosen. Incredibly, the next year he gave the Rangers a 20-7 record, although it was the sort of 20-win season that underscores the almost non-existent value of pitcher won-lost records—his ERA was 4.41, good for the crazy offensive environment of 1998, but hardly dominating. Helling cloned that season three times in the next three years, albeit without such a gaudy personal record.

YU DARVISH, RHP (2012-2016)
By 2011 the Rangers had come a long way from the team's early financial instability. When the Nippon Ham Fighters made the 25-year-old Darvish available during the 2011-2012 offseason, the Rangers won the right just to talk with him with an offer of $51,703,411, then signed him to a six-year contract worth an additional $56 million. He proved to be largely worth it (depending on how one judges what approximately $108 million should get you in horseflesh—we're not experienced with that sort of thing around here; we know it will get you an equivalent number of boxes of Kraft macaroni & cheese dinner totaling 48.8 million pounds), although his Arlington stay was interrupted by a partially torn elbow ligament and compounded by constant cavils that he should have been better for the money. Darvish and his large assortment of pitches were dealt to the Dodgers at the 2017 trade deadline. The rewards for that deal have yet to materialize, but he's continued to pitch well between injuries, with a career strikeout rate of 11.1 batters per nine.

A Taxonomy of 2020 Abnormalities

by Rob Mains

I'm going to start this with a trivia question. Trust me, it's relevant. Don't bother skipping to the end of the article to find the answer, it's not there.

Only five players have appeared in 140 or more games for 16 straight seasons. Who are they?

It's a trivia question starting off an essay, so you know how this works: Whatever you guessed, you're wrong. It's okay. As someone who purchased this book, chances are good that you're an educated baseball fan. But the circumstances behind 2020 force us to abandon, or at least seriously question, some of our favorite patterns and crutches for evaluating the game we love.

We just completed what was undoubtedly the strangest season in MLB history. No fans, geographically limited schedule, universal DH, seven-inning twin bills, runners on second in extra innings, a 16-team postseason, a club playing at a Triple-A stadium. Some of these changes will likely persist (sorry), but we've never had so many tweaks dumped on us all at once, at least not since they figured out how many balls were in a walk.

And the biggest, of course, was the 60-game season. The 19th century was dotted with teams that went bankrupt before the season ended, but the lone season with only 60 scheduled games was 1877. That year there were only six teams, the league rostered a total of 77 players (just 16 more than the 2020 Marlins), and batters called for pitches to be thrown high or low by the pitcher, who was 50 feet away. We can say the 2020 season was easily the shortest ever for recognizable baseball.

As such, it'll stand out. Few abbreviated seasons do. Just about everybody reading this knows the 1994 season ended after Seattle's Randy Johnson struck out Oakland's Ernie Young for the last out of the Mariners-A's game on August 11. The ensuing player strike wiped out the rest of the season and the postseason. Teams played only 112-117 games that year.

And many of you know that a strike in the middle of the 1981 season split the season in two, resulting in the only Division Series until 1995. Teams played only 103-111 games that year, the shortest regular season since 1885.

Those two seasons are memorable. So when we see that nobody drove in 100 runs in 1981, or that Greg Maddux was the only pitcher with 180 or more innings pitched in 1994, we think, "Of course. Strike year."

But we don't remember other short years. You might not recall that the 1994 strike spilled into the next year, chopping 18 games off the 1995 schedule. You might've read that the 1918 season, played during the last pandemic, ended after Labor Day due to the government's World War I "work or fight" order. A strike erased the first week and a half of the 1972 season, but that year's best known as the last time pitchers batted in the American League.

The point is, while we don't remember small changes to the schedule, we remember the big ones. The 1981 mid-season strike. The 1994 season- and Series-ending strike. And, of course, the pandemic-shortened 2020 season. We won't need a reminder why Marcell Ozuna's 18 homers were the fewest to lead the National League in a century. (Literally; Cy Williams led with 15 in 1920.)

Now, about that trivia question. The five players are Hank Aaron, Brooks Robinson, Pete Rose, Ichiro Suzuki, and Johnny Damon. The one nobody gets, of course, is Damon, and a lot of people miss Ichiro, whose last season of 140-plus games came garbed in the red-orange and ocean blue of Miami when he was 42. That's half of what makes it a good question. The other half is the two guys whom many think made the list but didn't. Lou Gehrig? His streak started in the Yankees' 42nd game of the 1925 season and lasted only 13 seasons after that. And everybody assumes Cal Ripken Jr. did it, having played 2,632 straight games over 17 seasons. But one of those 17 seasons was 1994, when the Orioles played only 112 games.

My point? *I just told you* everybody remembers the 1994 strike year, but everybody forgets it fell in the middle of Ripken's streak, separating the first twelve years from the last four. Just because we recall something doesn't mean it's always at the front of our minds.

Nobody is going to forget 2020, and baseball is obviously not the main reason. But there will come a time in the future when you're looking at a player's or a team's record, and there will be baffling numbers there for 2020, and you'll think, "I wonder what happened." (Not to mention the missing line for minor league players.) Just like you forgot that the 1994 strike limited Ripken to 112 games.

Try not to forget it, though. The 2020 season resulted in weird statistical results for several reasons.

There were only 60 games.
I know, duh. But that had impacts beyond counting stats like Ozuna's home run total or Yu Darvish and Shane Bieber leading the majors with eight wins. (I know, pitcher wins, but still.)

The 162-game season is the longest among major North American sports, and that duration gives us a gift. Over the course of a long season, small variations tend to even out. A player who has a ten-game hot streak will probably have a ten-game cold streak. A team that starts the year losing a bunch of close games will probably win a bunch of them. We get regression to the mean. Statistics stabilize.

Consider flipping a coin. Over the long run, we expect it to come up heads about half the time. But the fewer flips, the more variation there'll be. If you flip a coin six times, probability theory tells us you'll get at least two-third heads about 34 percent of the time. Flip it 30 times, your chance of two-thirds heads drops to five percent.

Or, relevant to this case, if you flip a coin 60 times, your chance of getting at least 36 heads—that's 60 percent—is 7.75 percent. Expand the coin-flipping to 162 times, and the chance of getting 60 percent heads drops to 0.73 percent.

In other words, the odds of an outcome that's 20 percent better (or worse) than expected is *more than ten times higher* when you flip your coin 60 times than when you do it 162 times. Call it small sample size, call lack of mean reversion, or call it luck not evening out, 162 is a lot more predictive than 60. You get much more variation over 60 games than over 162. Bieber's 1.63 ERA and 0.87 FIP aren't something we'd see over a full season, and neither is Javier Baéz's .203/.238/.360.

Some players' lines in 2020 look normal. Brian Anderson had an .811 OPS in 2019 and an .810 OPS in 2020. (He probably would have gotten that last point if he'd been given enough time.) But there are many like Bieber and Baéz, some of them from young players still establishing their talent levels. The answer to the question, "What went right or wrong for that guy in 2020?" is most likely "Nothing, it was just a 2020 thing."

Preseason training was abbreviated for hitters.
Every year, spring training drags. Players get tired of it, fans get tired of it, and you sure can tell sportswriters get tired of it. Yes, something to get everyone into shape is necessary, but does it really have to drag on for over a month? Can't we shorten it?

The 2020 season answered in the negative, at least for hitters. Warren Spahn is credited with saying that hitting is timing and pitching is upsetting timing. It appears nobody had his timing down after the abbreviated July summer camp. Through August 9—18 games into the season—MLB batters were hitting .230/.311/.395 with a .275 BABIP. That BABIP, had it held, would have been the lowest since 1968, the Year of the Pitcher. In recent years it's hovered around .300.

It didn't hold. Play returned to more normal levels the rest of the year: .249/.325/.425 with a .297 BABIP starting August 10. But batters whose play concentrated in those first two weeks wound up with ugly lines. Andrew

Benintendi went on the injured list with a season-ending rib cage strain on August 11. His final line: .103/.314/.128 in 14 games. Franchy Cordero went on the IL with a hamate bone fracture on August 9 and a .154/.185/.231 line. Even though he came back strong in a late September return, it was too late to repair his full-season numbers.

Preseason training was abbreviated for pitchers.

Every year, spring training drags. Players get tired of it, fans get tired of it … wait, I already said that. But the abbreviated preseason was tough on pitchers, too. As noted, they had the upper hand coming out of the gate. But then they lost that hand. And then their arms, too.

The 2020 season was spread over 67 days. During those 67 days, 237 pitchers hit the Injured List, compared to 135 in the first 67 days of 2019. A lot of those IL stints, though, were COVID-19-related. Still, over the first 67 days of the 2019 season, there were 72 pitchers on the IL with arm injuries. That figure jumped to 110 in 2020, a 53 percent increase.

There are a number of factors contributing to pitcher arm injuries, ranging from usage to velocity, but it appears that attenuated preseason training played a role. A lot of pitchers had super-short seasons due to arm woes. Corey Kluber, Roberto Osuna, and Shohei Ohtani combined for seven innings, none after August 8. All suffered arm injuries. We'll never know whether they'd have fared better with a longer preseason, but we can guess how they probably feel.

Everybody played.

Rosters were set to expand from 25 to 26 in 2020, so even if we'd had a normal season, we'd have likely seen 2019's record of 1,410 players on MLB rosters broken. But due to the pandemic, rosters started the year at 30 and were cut to only 28. Add multiple COVID-19 absences and the revolving door caused by poor starts by hitters and a rash of pitcher arm injuries, and 1,289 players appeared in MLB games in 2020. The comparable figure over the first 67 days of the 2019 season was 1,109. That 16 percent increase works out to an average of six more players per team in 2020 compared to a similar slice of 2019. A future look back at 2020 rosters will include a lot of unfamiliar names.

Plus became a minus.

In advanced metrics, we adjust batter and pitcher performance for park and league/era variations. A plus sign appended to the end of a measure means that it's adjusted for park and league. It's scaled to an average of 100, with higher figures above average and lower figures below average. (Similarly, a metric with a minus is also park- and league-adjusted and scaled to 100, with lower values better.) Here at BP, our advanced measure of offensive performance is DRC+. Baseball-Reference has OPS+ and FanGraphs has wRC+.

Using park and league adjustments, we can compare Dante Bichette's 1995 Steroid Era season at pre-humidor Coors Field (.340/.364/.620, 40 homers, 128 RBI, MVP runner-up) with Jim Wynn's 1968 Year of the Pitcher season at the cavernous Astrodome (.269/.376/.474, 26 homers, 67 RBI, no MVP votes). It's not close. DRC+, OPS+, and wRC+ all give the nod to Wynn, handily. This is a useful tool. As my Baseball Prospectus colleague Patrick Dubuque tweeted last fall, "Please note that when I ask how you are, I am already adjusting for era."

The 2020 season messes up plus (and minus) stats for two reasons. First, the park adjustment was based on only 30 home games instead of the usual 81. Everything noted above regarding the short season applies, literally doubly, to park effect calculations. DRC+ uses a single-season park factor. OPS+ uses a three-year average and wRC+ five years. The figure for 2020 is suspect.

Second, OPS+ and wRC+ adjust for league: American and National. (DRC+ adjusts for opponent, regardless of league.) While there were two leagues in 2020, they were an artificial construct. To reduce travel, teams played opponents geographically, not based on league. There weren't two leagues, American and National. There were three, Western, Central, and Eastern.

That makes a difference because teams in the same league played in different run-scoring environments. AL teams scored 4.58 runs per game, NL teams 4.71. That's a small difference. But teams in the East scored 0.21 more runs per game (4.95) than teams in the West (4.74), and they both scored a lot more than Central teams (4.25). Adjusting for league misses that difference, so this book will be safe in that regard, but other sources may be distorted somewhat.

Not every game was a "game."
In 2020, the rising tide of strikeouts was finally stemmed. Strikeouts per team per game fell from 8.8 in 2019 to 8.7 in 2020. That marked the first decline after 14 straight annual increases.

In 2020, the rising tide of strikeouts rose higher. Batters struck out in 23.4 percent of plate appearances compared to 23.0 percent in 2019. That marked the 15th straight annual increase.

Both are true statements.

Because of two rule changes—seven-inning doubleheaders and runners on second in extra innings—games in 2020 were unprecedented in their brevity. There were 37.0 plate appearances per game in 2020. The only years with fewer were 1904 and 1906-1909. The average game in 2020 entailed 8.61 innings pitched, the fewest since 1899.

So when you see any per-game stats for 2020, you need to increase them by 3 or 4 percent to get them on equal footing with recent years.

Texas Rangers 2021

Or, better, just ignore them. Last year happened. There were major league games contested between major league teams. But when you're looking at those physical or electronic baseball cards, when you're weaving narratives over why this young player's inevitable rise to stardom fell apart or why that old veteran rekindled his magic, don't linger on the 2020 line. It was just too weird.

Thanks to Lucas Apostoleris for research assistance.

—Rob Mains is an author of Baseball Prospectus.

Tranches of WAR

by Russell A. Carleton

We ask "replacement level" to be a lot of things. Sometimes contradictory things. Sometimes I wonder if we know what it even means anymore. The original idea was that it represented the level of production that a team could expect to get from "freely available talent", including bench players, minor leaguers, and waiver wire pickups. It created a common benchmark to compare everyone to, and for that reason, it represented an advancement well beyond what was available at the time. In fact, it created a language and a framework for evaluating players that was not just better but *entirely* different than what came before it.

But then we started mumbling in that language. The idea behind "wins above replacement" was one part sci-fi episode and one part mathematical exercise. Imagine that a player had disappeared before the season and suddenly, in an alternate timeline, his team would have had to replace him. The distance between him and that replacement line was his value. We need to talk about that alternate timeline.

Without getting too into 2:00 am "deep conversations" with extensive navel-gazing, it's worth thinking about why one player might not be playing, while another might.

- A player might not be playing because he has a short-term injury or his manager believes that he needs a day off.
- A player might not be playing because he has a longer-term injury that requires him to be on the injured list.

There's a difference here between these two situations. In particular, the first one generally *doesn't* involve a compensatory roster move, while the second one does. It's possible, though not guaranteed, that the person who will be replacing the injured/resting player would be the same in either case. That matters. Teams generally carry a spare part for all eight position players on the diamond, although in the era of a four-player bench, those spare parts usually are the backup plan for more than one spot.

Texas Rangers 2021

A couple of years ago, I posed a hypothetical question. Suppose that a team had two players in its system fighting for a fourth outfielder spot. One of them was a league average hitter, but would be worth 20 runs below average if allowed to play center field for a full season. One of them was a perfectly average fielder, but would be 15 runs below average as a hitter, if allowed to play an entire season. Which of the two should the team roster? It's tempting to say the second one, as overall, he is the better player. That misses the point. A league average hitter on the bench isn't just a potential replacement for an injured outfielder. He might also pinch hit for the light-hitting shortstop in a key spot. You keep the average hitter on the roster, even though he isn't a hand-in-glove fit for one specific place on the field, because being a bench player is a different job description than being a long-term fill-in for someone. If you find yourself in need of a longer-term fill-in, you can bring the other guy up from AAA.

When we're determining the value of an everyday player though, if he had disappeared before the season and a team would have had to replace his production, they likely would have done it with a player who was a long-term fill-in type because they would have had to replace a guy who played everyday. Maybe that's the same guy that they would have rostered on their bench anyway, but we don't know. It gets to the query of what we hope to accomplish with WAR. Are we looking for an accurate modeling of reality or are we looking for a common baseline to compare everyone to? Both have their uses, but they are somewhat different questions.

Let's talk about another dichotomy.

- A player might not be playing because he isn't very good and is a bench-level player.
- A player might not be playing because there is another player on the team who has a situational advantage that makes him the better choice today. The classic case of this is a handedness platoon. On another day, he might be a better choice.

When we think about player usage, I think we're still stuck in the model that there are starters and there are scrubs. We have plenty of words for bench players or reserves or backups or utility guys. We do still have the word "platoon" in our collective vocabulary, but in the age of short benches, it's hard to construct one. It's always been hard to construct them. You have to find two players who hit with different hands, have skill sets that complement each other, and probably play the same position. In the era of the short bench, one of them had probably better double as a utility player in some way. Baseball has a two-tiered language geared toward the idea of regulars and reserves. The fact that it was so easy for me to find plenty of synonyms for "a player whose primary function is to come into a game to replace a regular player if he is injured or resting" should tell you something.

I'm always one to look for "unspoken words" in baseball. What is it called when someone is both half of a platoon and the utility infielder? That guy exists sometimes, but he reveals himself in that role—usually by accident. We don't have a word for that, and whenever I find myself saying "we don't have a word for that", I look for new opportunities. What do you call it, further, when the job of being the utility infielder is decentralized across the whole infield with occasional contributions from the left fielder? It's not even a "super-utility" player. What happens when you build your entire roster around the idea that everyone will be expected to be a triple major?

⚾ ⚾ ⚾

I think someone else beat me to this one, and on a grand scale. Platoons work because we know that hitters of the opposite hand to the pitcher get better results than hitters of the same hand, usually to the tune of about 20 points of OBP. If you want to express that in runs, it usually comes out to somewhere around 10 to 12 runs of linear weights value prorated across 650 PA. But hang on a second, now let's say that we have two players who might start today, both of roughly equal merit with the bat. One has a handedness advantage, but is the worse fielder of the two. In that case, as long as his "over the course of a season" projection as a fielder at whatever position you want to slot him into is less than a 10-run drop from the guy he might replace, then he's a better option today.

We're not used to thinking of utility players as bat-first options, who would play below-average defense at three different infield positions. That guy might hook on as a 2B/3B/LF type (Howie Kendrick, come on down!) but teams usually think to themselves that they need as their utility infielder someone who "can handle" shortstop, the toughest of the infield spots to play. If someone can do that *and* hit well, he's probably already starting somewhere, so he's not available as a utility infielder. It's easier for those glove guys to find a job. In a world where the replacement for a shortstop *has to be* the designated utility infielder, that makes sense.

But as we talked about last week, we're living in a different world. The rate at which a replacement for a regular starter turns out to be *another starter* shifting over to cover has gone way up over the last five years. There was always some of it in the game, but this has been a supernova of switcheroos. Now if your second baseman is capable of playing a decent shortstop, that 2B/3B/LF guy can swap in. He's not actually playing shortstop, and maybe the defense suffers from the switch, but if he's got enough of a bat, he might outhit those extra fielding miscues. And in doing so, he is effectively your backup shortstop.

Somewhere along the lines, teams got hip to the idea of multi-positional play from their regulars. I've written before about how you can't just put a player, however athletic, into a new position and expect much at first. The data tell us that. Eventually, players can learn to be multi-positionalists, but it takes time, roughly on the order of two months, before they're OK. But there's a hidden message in there. If you give a player some reps at a new spot, he's a reasonably gifted athlete and somewhat smart and willing to learn, he could probably pick it up enough to get to "good enough," and it doesn't take forever. You just have to be purposeful about it. Maybe you get to the point where you can start to say "he's still below average but we could move him there and get another bat into the lineup, and it's a net win."

Teams have started to build those extra lessons into their player development program. It used to be seen as a mark of weakness to be relegated to "utility player" because that meant that you were a bench player (all those synonyms above come with a side of stigma). Now, it's a way of building a team. If you get a few reps in the minors (where it doesn't count) at a spot, you'll have at least played the spot at game speed before. There are limits to how far you can push that. A slow-footed "he's out in left field because we don't have the DH" guy is never going to play short, but maybe your third baseman can try second base and not look like a total moose out there.

⚾ ⚾ ⚾

Back to WAR. I'd argue that the world of starters and scrubs is slowly disintegrating, for good cause. In the event that a regular starter really does go down with an injury–ostensibly, the alternate universe scenario that WAR is attempting to model–it makes the team a little more resilient to replacing him. And the good news is that you're more likely to be able to replace him with the best of the bench bunch, rather than the third-best guy, because the best guy doesn't have to be an exact positional match for the guy who got hurt. And that's what the manager would want to do. He'd want to replace that long-term production, not with an amalgam of everyone else who played that position, but with the best guy available from his reserves.

Now this is still WAR. We still want to retain the principle that we should be measuring a player, and not his teammates. We need some sort of common baseline, and despite what I just said, we'll still need some sort of amalgam. To construct that, I give to you the idea of the tranche. The word, if you've not heard it before, refers to a piece of a whole that is somehow segmented off. It's often used in finance to talk about layers of a financial instrument.

Here, I want you to consider that there are 30 starters at each of the seven non-battery positions (catchers should have their own WAR, since only a catcher can replace a catcher). We can identify them by playing time, and we can futz around with the definition a little bit if we need to. Next, among those who aren't in that starting pool, we identify the top tranche of the 30 best bench players, which I would again identify by playing time, and then the second and third and fourth and so on. If a player were to disappear, his manager would probably want to take a guy from that top tranche of the bench to replace him. In a world where even the starters can slide around the field, that becomes more feasible.

We can take a look at that top tranche and say "How many of them showed that they are able to play (first, second, etc.)?" and therefore could have directly substituted for the starter? How many of them could have been a direct substitute for our injured player? We don't know whether one of them would be on *a specific* team, but we can say that 40 percent of the time, a manager would have been able to draw from tranche 1 in filling the role, and 35 percent from tranche 2. But on tranche 1, we can also look at how many of those players played a position that could have then shifted and covered for that spot. We'd need some eligibility criteria for all of this (probably a minimum number of games played) but it would just be a matter of multiplication. Shortstop would be harder to fill, and managers would probably be dipping a little further down in the talent pool, and so replacement level would be lower, as it is now.

Doing some quick analysis, I found that the difference in just batting linear weights (haven't even gotten into running or fielding) between tranche 1 and tranche 2 in 2019 was about 6.5 runs, prorated across 650 PA. Between tranche 1 and tranche 3, it's 10.8 runs. The ability to shift those plate appearances up the ladder has some real value.

This part is important. We can also give credit to starters for the positions that they showed an ability to play, even if they didn't play them (this is the guy fully capable of playing center, but who's in a corner because the team already has a good center fielder) because he allows a team to carry a player who hits like a left fielder to functionally be the team's backup center fielder. He facilitates that movement upward among the tranches. We can start to appreciate the difference between a left fielder who would never be able to hack it in center (and the compensatory move that his team would have to make) and the left fielder who could do it, but just didn't have to very often.

Past that, you can continue to use whatever hitting and fielding and running metrics you like to determine a player's value, but when we get down to constructing that baseline, I'd argue we need a better conceptual and mathematical framework. It's going to require some more #GoryMath than we're used to, but I'd argue it's a better conceptualization of the way that MLB actually plays the game in 2020. If…y'know…MLB plays in 2020. If WAR is going to be our flagship statistic among the *acronymati*, then we need to acknowledge that it contains some old and starting-to-be-out-of-date assumptions about the game. We may need to tinker with it. Here's my idea for how. ■

—*Russell A. Carleton is an author of Baseball Prospectus.*

Secondhand Sport

by Patrick Dubuque

Back before time stopped, I liked to go to thrift stores. Now that I'm older, I rarely ever buy anything—I don't need much in my life, now—but I still enjoy the old familiar circuit: check to see if there are baseball cards to write about, look for board or card games to play with the kids, scan for random ironic jerseys, hit the book section. It takes ten, maybe fifteen minutes. Thrift stores are the antithesis of modern online shopping, because you don't know what they have, and you don't even really know what you want. It's junk, literal junk, stuff other people thought was worthless. That's what makes it great.

In an idealized economy, thrift stores shouldn't exist. Everybody has a living wage, and every product has a durability that exactly matches its desired life; nothing should need to be given away, no one should need to be given to. But then, thrift stores shouldn't work on a customer experience level, either. You wouldn't think an ethos of "let's make everything disorganized and hard to find" would lead to customer satisfaction, but low-budget retailers like TJ Maxx and Ross thrive on this model. People like bargain hunting as much for the hunting as the bargain; it's part of the experience, spending time as if it's a wager. There's a thrill, occasionally, in inefficiency.

In sports, the modern overuse of the word "inefficiency" is a condemnation: It insinuates that there is *an* efficiency, a correct way to be found, and that all other ways are wrong ways. It's prevalent in baseball but hardly contained to it; the lifehack, the Silicon Valley disruption are other examples of productivity creep in our daily lives. Their modern success makes plenty of sense. Maximization of resources, after all, is its own puzzle, and an industry of European board games is founded upon it. It's fun to take a system and optimize it, unravel it like a sudoku puzzle. If there's only one kind of genius, after all, there's no way anyone can fail to appreciate it.

Baseball has been hacking away at these perceived inefficiencies since its inception: platoons, bullpens, farm systems were all installed to extract more out of the tools at hand. But it's been a particular badge of the sabermetric movement, from Ken Phelps and his All-Star Team to Ricardo Rincon and the darlings of *Moneyball*. It's business, but it's also an ethos: the idea that there's treasure among the trash, something we all failed to appreciate until someone brought it to light.

It's the myth that made Sidd Finch so enticing, that fuels so many "best shape" narratives and new pitch promises. We all, athletes and unathletic sportswriters, want to believe that there's genius trapped inside us, and that it's just a matter of puzzling out the combination to unlock it. That our art, our style is the next inefficiency, waiting for our own Billy Beane. It's why we root for underdogs, and why we're excited for the Mike Tauchmans and the Eurubiel Durazos, champions of skin-deep mediocrity.

Except we aren't anymore, really. The days of "Free X" have descended beyond the ring of irony and into obscurity. There are still Xs to be freed, or at least one X, duplicated endlessly: Mike Ford, Luke Voit, Max Muncy. The undervalued one-dimensional slugger demonstrated how the game hasn't quite culturally caught up to its logical extreme. But for those who don't fit the rather spacious mold, times are grimmer. As Rob Arthur revealed several months ago, there's been a marked increase in the number of sub-replacement relievers. It's the outcome of a greater number of teams forced to play out games without the talent to win them, but it's also emblematic of the modern tendency of teams to dispose of their disposable assets, burning through cost-controlled arms the way that man chopped down forests in *The Lorax*. Stuff just isn't built to outlive their original owners anymore.

It's unsurprising, given how well-mined the market for inefficiencies has been of late. The disciples of the early analytics departments, and the disciples of those, have proliferated the league, with only a few backwater holdouts. The league has grown smarter, but every team has learned the same lesson. In fact, the phenomenon creates a peculiar kind of feedback loop: As teams value a specific subset of players or skills, prospective athletes learn to increase their own marketability by conforming themselves to the demands of their prospective employers.

And that's tragic, in the way that the extinction of animals is tragic; a certain amount of biodiversity in baseball has been lost. Shortstops hit like outfielders. Pitchers don't hit at all. Only the catchers remain idiosyncratic, thanks to the defensive demands of their position; eventually they too will be required to produce like everyone else, or they'll meet the fate of their battery mates. A perfect economy requires perfect production.

I mentioned earlier that more and more, I leave thrift stores empty-handed. It is true that I am more discerning than in the past; my bookshelves are full, and there are more streaming films than I will ever be able to watch. But there are other factors at play.

Thrift stores are, in a way, the bond markets of retail. When the economy is rough and other retailers are struggling, more people look secondhand for their products. But as recently as last year, publications were noting a reversal of the trend: Companies like Goodwill and Savers were expanding despite a strong economy. Publications credited a heightened sense of environmentalism and a rejection of cutting-edge fashion as drivers behind the increase, though the more likely answer is the modern American economy hasn't showered its favors equally, particularly among the young.

But it is more than just the economy. Baseball and thrift stores share something else in common, evident in our current conversations about re-starting the sport: They live in the gray area between public service and private enterprise. Thrift stores provide affordable necessities to lower-class citizens, and collectibles and fashion for the middle-class. Because of the success of the latter, prices have gone up across the board. Especially in terms of clothing, the middle-class flight from fashion into vintage has instead carried the aftereffects of fashion, including its costs, into a territory where people just want clothes. But there's another factor in the rise of prices, in the form of the internet.

The Goodwills of the world have grown smarter, too, employing the internet to extract full value from their detritus. Ebay, similarly, has lost much of the charm it had as a new frontier around the turn of the century. Everything has a price point now; even individual taste is no match for the algorithm, because anything rare, no matter how niche its market, is a collectible to someone.

The internet has had the same effect on thrift stores that sabermetrics has had on baseball; its equivalent to OBP was the bar scanner. As detailed in Slate, the rise of second-party stores on eBay and Amazon birthed an entire industry of used-good salespeople, armed with PDAs and scanners, buying books for three dollars to sell online for five. The author, Michael Savitz, reports earning $60,000 by working nearly 80 hours a week; he makes it clear that this is not a vocation of his choosing. It's long hours, with no real creativity or individuality, skimming the cream off of a local establishment and flipping it to someone with a little more money on the other side of the country. And once the vocation exists, the obvious question arises: why wait to put the wares out on the shelves? Why allow value to exist at all?

Nothing is ruined. Thrift stores will continue to sell polo shirts and DVDs, and baseball will continue to exist and make or lose money, depending on who you believe. But as we continue to refine our knowledge, we lose something in the conquest for efficiency, a delight born out of the unknown. The problem isn't the efficiency itself; we can't blame the booksellers, or the people sweeping freeways to collect grams of platinum from damaged catalytic converters. The problem is a system that requires this sort of profit-skimming behavior in order to feed families (or, for corporations, maximize shareholder return).

Texas Rangers 2021

In times like these, with the 2020 season on the brink and the collective bargaining agreement close behind, it can often feel like the current situation is untenable. It can't keep going like this, even if we don't know what to do about it. But as with thrift stores, there's an equally irresistible feeling that it *has* to keep going, that it would be unimaginable to not have this broken, amazing sport. Both industries exist on an invisible foundation of friction, of chaos and unpredictability, even as both see their foundations buffed down to a perfect, untouchable polish. But if COVID-19 and its financial ramifications do, as some have suggested, make it such that the baseball that returns is fundamentally different than the baseball that came before, perhaps this is the time to lean in, and change the game even more. Fix bunting. Make defense more difficult. Create viable, alternate strategies. Add some chaos back into baseball. It's fun when no one knows quite where things are.

—Patrick Dubuque is an author of Baseball Prospectus.

Steve Dalkowski Dreaming

by Steven Goldman

We dream of being a pitcher, of starring in the major leagues. Depending on your age and your sense of historical perspective, you might imagine yourself as Walter Johnson, throwing harder than anyone else—hitting more batters than anyone else, too, but always feeling bad about it. You could picture yourself as a Tom Seaver or a David Cone, with all the stuff in the world but still being cerebral about it, thinking about so much more than burning 'em in there. There are so many models one could choose: You could be a Lefty Gomez, Jim Bouton, or Bill Lee, skilled, but not taking the whole thing too seriously, or a Lefty Grove, Bob Gibson, or Steve Carlton, powerful but treating each start like a mission to be survived instead of a game to be enjoyed.

Very few would dream of being Steve Dalkowski, the former Baltimore Orioles prospect who died of COVID-19 last week at the age of 80. Yet, there is something just as noble in Dalkowski's negative accomplishments—and accomplishments is what they are—as there is in the precision-engineered pitching of a Greg Maddux. You have to be very good to be that bad. Dalkowski had all of the stuff of the greatest pitchers but none of the command; his story is not one of failing to conquer his limitations, but striving against one of the cruelest hands that fate or genetics or personality can deal us: A desire to achieve great things which is almost but not quite matched by the ability to meet that goal.

As with Johnson, Grove, Bob Feller, and the rest of the hard-throwing pitchers who played before the advent of modern radar guns, we have to take the word of the players and coaches who saw Dalkowski pitch as to his velocity. He was a hard-drinking, maximum-effort pitcher who, if their memories are to be believed, consistently threw over 100 miles per hour. His was the Maltese Fastball, the stuff that dreams are made of. The problem is that velocity without command and control is still a good distance from utility. Dalkowski was the most effective towel you could design for a fish, the sleekest bathing suit intended to be worn by an astronaut, but that doesn't mean he wasn't beautiful: We can appreciate a journey even if it doesn't end at the intended destination.

Whether because of sloppy mechanics he couldn't calm, an inability to understand that a consistent 98 in the strike zone would likely be more effective than a consistent 110 out of it, or all that beer, Dalkowski could never make the adjustments that pitchers like Feller and Nolan Ryan made before him, possibly because he had so far to go: Feller, who never pitched in the minors, came up at 17 and spent three years walking almost seven batters per nine innings before settling in at 3.8 beginning when he was 20. Ryan started out walking over six batters per nine but gradually improved as his long career played out; for him to go from 6.2 walks per nine with the 1966 Greenville Mets to 3.7 with the 1989 Texas Rangers represents a 40 percent reduction. An equivalent improvement by Dalkowski would still have left him walking over 11 batters per nine innings.

Dalkowski was like *The Room* of pitchers, a player so bad he became good again. Cal Ripken, Sr., who both played with and managed Dalkowski, recalled in a 1979 *Sporting News* "where are they now" piece the occasion when the pitcher crossed up his catcher and his fastball, "hit the plate umpire smack in the mask. The mask broke all to pieces and the umpire wound up in the hospital for three days with a concussion. If they ever had a radar gun in those days, I'll bet Dalkowski would have been timed at 110 miles an hour."

Signed by the Orioles out of New Britain High in Connecticut in 1957, Dalkowski was sent to Kingsport in the Appalachian League, where he pitched 62 innings. He allowed only 22 hits in 62 innings, or 3.2 per nine, a number with no equivalent in major league history (though Aroldis Chapman came close in 2014), and also struck out 121 (17.6 per nine) and walked 129 (18.7). He was also charged with 39 wild pitches. That June, one of his fastballs clipped a Dodgers prospect named Bob Beavers and carried away part of his ear. "The first pitch was over the backstop, the second pitch was called a strike, I didn't think it was," Beavers said last year. "The third pitch hit me and knocked me out, so I don't remember much after that. I couldn't get in the sun for a while, and I never did play baseball again." Former minor leaguer Ron Shelton based the *Bull Durham* pitcher Nuke LaLoosh on Dalkowski. And yet, to see him as a figure of fun, an amusing loser, is to misunderstand something unique and strange.

Dalkowski kept on posting some of the strangest lines in baseball history. Pitching for the Stockton Ports of the Class C California League in 1960, he struck out 262 and walked 262 in 170 innings. Yet, he did improve, especially after pitching for Earl Weaver at Elmira in 1962. Weaver had previously had Dalkowski at Aberdeen in 1959, but wasn't ready to grapple with him then. This time he was. "I had grown more and more concerned about players with great physical abilities who could not learn to correct certain basic deficiencies no matter how much you instructed or drilled them," he related in his autobiography, *It's What You Learn After You Know It All That Counts*. He got permission from the Orioles to give all of his players the Stanford-Binet IQ test. "Dalkowski finished in the 1 percentile in his ability to understand facts. Steve, it was said to say, had the ability to do everything but learn." [sic]

IQ tests are problematic diagnostic tools, so take Weaver's estimate of Dalkowski's mental capabilities with a grain of salt. What's important is that even if he got to the right answer by way of the wrong reason, Weaver had learned something valuable. His insight was to stop asking Dalkowski to learn new pitches and just let him get by with the two that he had. Were Dalkowski a prospect today, that would have been a no-brainer: Can't develop a third pitch? The bullpen is right over there, sir. Player development wasn't like that then, but Weaver, temporarily Dalkowski's mentor, could let him work with what he had. According to Weaver, the pitcher responded: "In the final 57 innings he pitched that season Dalkowski gave up 1 earned run, struck out 110 batters, and walked only 11." It's not true—as per the *Elmira Star-Gazette*, as of late July, Dalkowski had walked 71 in 106 innings and finished with 114 in 160 innings, which means Dalkowski's control actually faded at the end of the season rather than improved—but that doesn't mean it didn't happen in some sense, just that it didn't happen that way. Again, it's the journey, not the destination, and his ERA was 3.04 so *something* had gone right.

Also along the way: The next spring, Orioles manager Billy Hitchcock was rooting for Dalkowski to make the team as a long-man—maybe Weaver had gotten through to him. There were things out of Weaver's control, like the universe's twisted sense of humor: that March, Dalkowski's elbow went "twang."

You sometimes read that it was the Orioles' insistence on Dalkowski learning the curve that did him in, but even if they hadn't learned their lesson, the injury was probably just a coincidence: Dalkowski had thrown an incredible number of pitches over the previous few years. Still, it testifies to the dangers of trying to get what you want and risking the loss of what you had. Dalkowski tried to come back, but the 110-mph stuff was gone. A pitcher with no control and no stuff is…a civilian. What followed were years of vagabond living, arrests for drunkenness. There were Alcoholics Anonymous meetings, assistance from baseball alumni associations, but none of it took. From the 1990s until the time of his passing he dwelt in an assisted living facility, suffering from alcohol-related dementia. He'd been a heavy drinker since his teenage years. As with all those pitches per game, there was a price to be paid. You make choices on the journey and some of them are irrevocable. It's like a fairy tale: "Bite of poison apple? Don't mind if I do."

In the aforementioned *Sporting News* profile, Chuck Stevens, the head of the Association of Professional Ballplayers of America, a ballplayer charity, said, "I've got nothing against drinking. I do it myself sometimes. But, I don't condone common drunkenness. We went through lots of heartache and many dollars, but Dalkowski didn't want to help himself and we weren't going to keep him drunk." The journey is *un*like a fairy tale: No one will come along and kiss it better, not if they're busy forming judgments.

In the end, we are left with a sort of philosophical chicken/egg conundrum: Is failing to meet your goals evidence of unfulfilled potential or the lack of it? Isn't what you did by definition what you were capable of doing? Or could you have broken through to something better with the right help, the right lucky break? These are unanswerable questions, and how we try to answer them may say more about us than about the people we're judging.

No pitcher ever has it easy. *All* pitchers must work hard. *All* pitchers must refine their craft. It's almost never just about *stuff*. Dalkowski dreaming is no insult to the great pitchers who made it; from Pete Alexander to Max Scherzer, they have all earned their way up. And yet, if it is true that we can only do as much as we can do, then the journey would be more of an adventure, the ultimate triumph or defeat more noble, if like Dalkowski we lacked 100 percent of the confidence, the command, the self-possession, the commitment, the resistance to making bad decisions that so many great players possess—to be gloriously human. Or, to put it more succinctly, it would be fun to be able to throw as hard as any person ever has. Even if just for a moment, and even if nothing more came of it than that, no one could say you hadn't lived life to the fullest.

—Steven Goldman is an author of Baseball Prospectus.

A Reward For A Functioning Society

by Cory Frontin and Craig Goldstein

On July 5, Nationals reliever Sean Doolittle said in the middle of a press conference regarding the restart of Major League Baseball and what would later be known as summer camp, "sports are like the reward of a functioning society." This sentence was amidst a much longer, thoughtful reply about the societal and health conditions under which MLB players were being brought back. It's a very similar sentiment to one Jane McManus used on April 7, when she discussed the White House's meeting with sports commissioners. She said "sports are the effect of a functioning society—not the precursor."

Both versions of the same sentiment spoke to a laudable ideal in the context of a country that was not addressing a rampaging virus, and opting instead to bring sports back for the feeling of normalcy rather than the reality of it. "Priorities," as McManus said.

On Wednesday, the NBA's Milwaukee Bucks conducted a wildcat/political strike, refusing to come out for Game 5 of their playoff series against the Orlando Magic. The Magic refused to accept the forfeit, and shortly thereafter other playoff series were threatened by player strikes. Eventually the league moved to postpone that day's games, folding to players leveraging their united power.

The backdrop against which these actions took place was the shooting by police of Jacob Blake. Blake was shot in the back seven times by police, as he attempted to get into his vehicle. He managed to survive the assault, but is paralyzed from the waist down.

⚾   ⚾   ⚾

The step taken to walk out, first by the Milwaukee Bucks, then subsequently by other NBA, WNBA, and MLB teams, was a step toward upholding the virtue of the sentiment described by McManus and Doolittle. But that sentiment does not align with the broad history of sports in this and other countries, a history that contradicts the core of the idealistic statement.

Sports have been a significant part of American society for most of its existence, expanding in importance and influence in recent years. The idea that society was functioning in a way that was worthy of the reward of sports for most of that time is laughable. Much of America is not functioning and has not functioned for Black people, full stop. The oppressed people at the center of this political act by players, specifically Black players, in concert throughout the NBA and in fits and starts throughout Major League Baseball, have not known a society that functions for them rather than *because* of them.

Politics has been part of the sports landscape since the inception of sport, but for just about as long people have bemoaned its presence. Sports are to be an escape, it is said. An escape from what, though? A functioning society?

No, the presence of sports has never signified a cultural or political system that is on the up and up. Rather, the presence of sports *reflect and reinforce the society* that produces them.

⚾ ⚾ ⚾

The Negro Leagues were born out of societal dysfunction. The need for entirely separate leagues, composed of Black and Latino players barred from the Major Leagues because of racism? That is not a functioning society, and yet there were sports.

Even the integration of players from the Negro Leagues resulted in a transfer of power and wealth from Black-owned businesses and communities and into white ones, mirroring the dysfunction that had bled into every aspect of American society at the time. Japheth Knopp noted in the Spring 2016 Baseball Research Journal:

> *The manner in which integration in baseball—and in American businesses generally—occurred was not the only model which was possible. It was likely not even the best approach available, but rather served the needs of those in already privileged positions who were able to control not only the manner in which desegregation occurred, but the public perception of it as well in order to exploit the situation for financial gain. Indeed, the very word integration may not be the most applicable in this context because what actually transpired was not so much the fair and equitable combination of two subcultures into one equal and more homogenous group, but rather the reluctant allowance—under certain preconditions—for African Americans to be assimilated into white society.*

To understand the value of a movement, though, is not to understand how it is co-opted by ownership, but to know the people it brings together and what they demand. When Jackie Robinson—the player who demarcated the inevitability of the end of the Negro leagues—attended the March on Washington for Jobs and Freedom in 1963, he did so with his family and marched alongside the people. He stood alongside hundreds of thousands to fight for their common civil and labor rights. "The moral arc of the universe is long," many freedom fighters have echoed, "but it bends towards justice." The bend, it is less frequently said, happens when a great mass of people place the moral arc of the universe on their knee and apply force, as Jackie, his family, and thousands of others did that day.

⚾   ⚾   ⚾

Of course, taking the moral arc of the universe down from the mantle and bending it is not without risk. Perhaps the outsized influence of athletes is itself a mark of a dysfunctional society, but, nonetheless, hundreds of athletes woke up on Wednesday morning with the power to bring in millions of dollars in revenues. That very power, as we would come to find out, was matched with the equal and opposite power to *not* bring those revenues. That power, in hands ranging from the Milwaukee Bucks, to Kenny Smith in the *Inside the NBA* Studio, from the unexpected ally, Josh Hader, and his largely white teammates to the notably Black Seattle Mariners, would be exercised for a single demand: the end to state violence against Black people. Not unlike the March itself, it sat at the intersection of the civil rights of Black Americans and bold labor action. The March on Washington stood in the face of a false notion of integration—against an integration of extraction but not one of equality—and proposed something different. Just the same, the acts of solidarity of August 26, 2020 will be remembered in stark defiance of MLB's BLM-branded, but ultimately empty displays on opening weekend.

Bold defiance like this can never be without risk. By choosing to exercise this power, the Milwaukee Bucks took a risk. They risked vitriol and backlash from those they disagreed with. They risked fines or seeing their contracts voided, as a walkout like this is prohibited by their CBA. They risked forfeiting a playoff game, one that, as the No. 1 seed in the playoffs, they'd worked all year to attain. They didn't know how Orlando would respond. It wasn't clear that other teams throughout the league would follow suit in solidarity. And it wasn't known the league would accept these actions and moderately co-opt them by "postponing" games that would have featured no players.

If the league reschedules the games, some of the athletes' risk—their shared sacrifice—will be diminished, in retrospect. But they did not know any of that when they took that risk. And it is often left to athletes to take these risks when others in society won't, especially those of their same socioeconomic status and levels of influence.

It is athletes, specifically BIPOC athletes, that take them, though, because they live with the risk of being something other than white in this country every day. They are no strangers to the realities of police brutality. It seems incongruous then, to say that sports are a reward for a functioning society when we rely on athletes to lead us closer to being a functioning society. Luckily, our beloved athletes, WNBA players first and foremost among them, understand what sports truly are: a pipebender for the moral arc of the universe.

—Craig Goldstein is editor in chief of Baseball Prospectus. Cory Frontin is an author of Baseball Prospectus.

Index of Names

Acosta, Maximo 72, 104
Acuna, Luisangel 73
Allard, Kolby 42
Anderson, Justin 84
Apostel, Sherten 74, 102
Arihara, Kohei 85
Benjamin, Wes 44
Brown, Zack 86
Burke, Brock 87
Butera, Drew 75
Calhoun, Willie 14
Carter, Evan 100
Chavez, Jesse 46
Choo, Shin-Soo 16
Cody, Kyle 48, 101
Crouse, Hans 88, 103
Dahl, David 18
Davis, Khris 20
DeShields, Delino 22
Dietrich, Derek 24
Dunning, Dane 50, 97
Evans, Demarcus 89
Foltynewicz, Mike 90
Foscue, Justin 75, 99
Gallo, Joey 26
Gibson, Kyle 52
Guzmán, Ronald 76
Hearn, Taylor 54
Heim, Jonah 77
Henriquez, Ronny 103
Herget, Jimmy 56
Hernández, Jonathan 58
Holt, Brock 28
Huff, Sam 78, 97
Jung, Josh 79, 96
Kiner-Falefa, Isiah 30
King, John 60
Leclerc, José 91
Lora, Bayron 80, 104
Lowe, Nate 80
Lyles, Jordan 62
Martin, Brett 64
Moss, Keithron 103
Nicasio, Juan 91
Odor, Rougned 32
Ornelas, Jonathan 103
Palumbo, Joe 92
Perdomo, Luis 66
Phillips, Tyler 93, 101
Rodríguez, Joely 68
Santana, Danny 81
Solak, Nick 34
Taveras, Leody 36, 95
Tejeda, Anderson 38, 100
Thompson, Bubba 82
Trevino, Jose 40
Vanasco, Ricky 102
Vincent, Nick 70
Walker, Steele 83
Weems, Avery 102
White, Eli 84
White, Owen 103

Winn, Cole 94, 98

For the Joy of Keeping Score

THIRTY81 Project is an ongoing graphic design project focused on the ballparks of baseball. Since being established in 2013, scorecards have been a fundemantal part of the effort. Each two-page card is uniquely ballpark-centric — there are 30 variants — and designed with both beginning and veteran scorekeepers in mind. Evolving over the years with suggestions from fans, broadcasters, and official scorers, the sheets are freely available to everyone as printable letter-size PDFs at the project webshop at www.THIRTY81Project.com

Download, Print, Score, Repeat ...

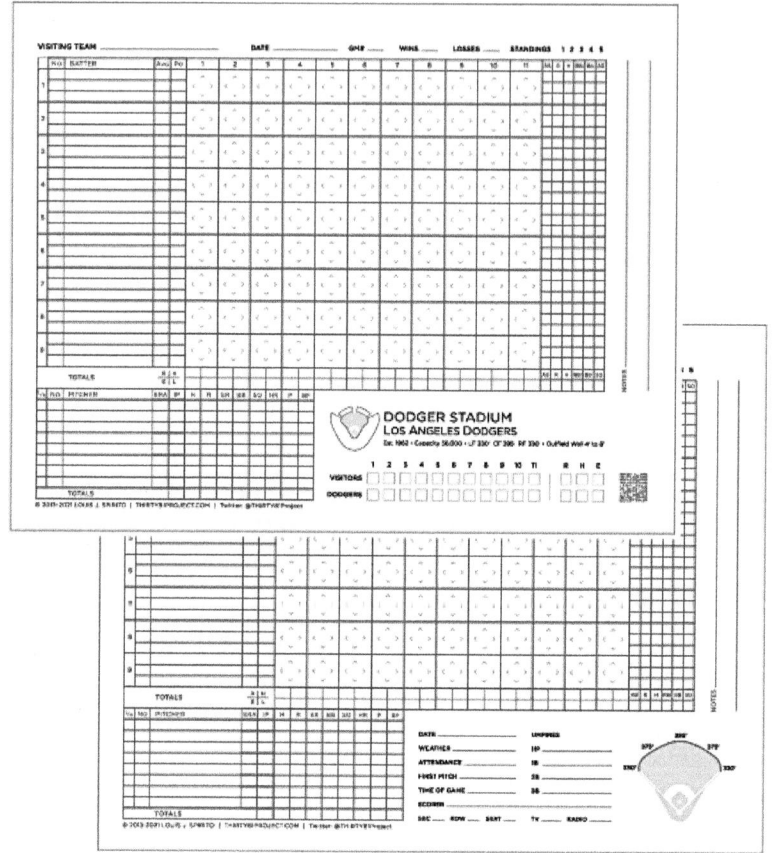

Scorecard design ©2013-2021 Louis J. Spirito | THIRTY81Project